ALLAN TAYLOR

THE SIX CORE VALUES OF SUNDAY SCHOOL

A Philosophical, Practical, &
Passionate Approach to Sunday School

FOREWORD BY
DR. JOHNNY HUNT

ACKNOWLEDGEMENTS

To my mom Mary Taylor...
   Who taught me to love Jesus, to love people, and who still
   prays daily for me.

To my Granny Shields Waller...
   Who taught me to love the Word of God and hide it in my
   heart.

To my twin brother Arden...
   Who has stretched me to new levels and challenged me to
   move beyond the status quo.

To Linda, my wife...
   Without her love, support, and constant sacrifice, my
   ministry and this book would be an impossibility.

To my children Kelly, Angie, and Jake . . .
   Each a precious gift from God.

ISBN 0-9706117-6-5

Design and Production
Riverstone Group, LLC, Canton, GA

Manuscript edited by Carolyn Cunningham

Scripture quotations are from the King James Bible unless noted otherwise.

Printed in Canada

CONTENTS

FOREWORD

When I think of building small groups in the context of the local church, no one comes to mind before Allan Taylor. Allan has as much passion and understanding of Sunday School and small groups as anyone I have ever met. It has been an absolute privilege to watch him as he has led the First Baptist Church of Woodstock to a new dimension of growth and depth in the Word of God.

The Lord has used him to build a solid leadership team and training team that I feel is second to none. I encourage the reading of this book by all those who have come to realize that "relationships" is the key word to reaching, keeping, and building of God's people. In this book, you will be enlightened, encouraged, and stretched concerning the main purpose of Sunday School. Allan will do an in-depth study of reaching, teaching, ministering, involving, assimilating, and building relationships with people.

It's been said that God loves people more than anything; and if people is what God loves, that's what the church of Jesus Christ should focus on. I have not found a better tool than Sunday School to seeing that truth become a reality. In these pages, you will learn sound, philosophical Sunday School principles and also be exposed to very practical applications of them. These newfound maxims will aid you as you care for the people God places under your watchcare.

Allan Taylor's heart burns for Sunday School. It will be evident to all that read it. This is must reading for anyone interested in developing an intentionally focused Sunday School ministry. Every Minister of Education should read this book; every Sunday School director should read it; and yes, every Sunday School teacher should be required to read it; and I can't think of a better training manual for new and potential Sunday School teachers. This book will help "equip the saints, for the work of the ministry." Read it and pass it on.

Dr. Johnny M. Hunt, Pastor
First Baptist Church
Woodstock, Georgia

INTRODUCTION

Over scores of years, Sunday School has been championed by many. Her flag has flown high above the church—like school colors flying over a college football stadium. But in recent years, some have attempted to take the flag down with a message that Sunday School is no longer relevant in the 21st century. Next to the personal commitment and involvement of her individual members, I believe Sunday School is still the best way to flesh out the Great Commission of our Lord Jesus Christ. I believe we have left many of the fundamentals that made Sunday School the proud entity she once was in our churches.

Before going into the ministry, I coached receivers and defensive backs as an assistant high school football coach at my alma mater, Fulton High School, in Knoxville, Tennessee. The ten years I spent coaching there taught me that blocking and tackling are what win games. So it is in church. The Sunday School that can block and tackle will be fruitful. To leave the fundamentals of Sunday School is to leave Sunday School. So let's not relinquish the fundamentals of a sound Sunday School ministry and then make declarations that Sunday School does not work! Nothing works if it is not worked!

My goal in this book is to once again establish the blocking and tackling of Sunday School. This book is not intended to be an exhaustive study of Sunday School methodologies. It is designed to present a philosophical base for Sunday School and then provide a few practices that have come from my experiences. I want this all to be done with a contagious passion for Sunday School. I am the product of a mother and grandmother who raised me; both loved Sunday School.

As I write, my mother is into her fifty-third year of teaching Sunday School. My grandmother lived from 1898-1985. Many of the older ladies in my home church used to tell me: "Allan, your grandmother was the best Bible teacher I have ever heard." As you can see, Sunday School is in my genes! Therefore, it is easy for me to be zealous about that which is so much a part of my heritage.

My love for Sunday School started as a boy where I was taken to Sunday School and church every Lord's Day. Every Saturday night, Mom would prepare me and my three brothers for church by making us take a bath, shine our shoes, and read our lesson from our Sunday School quarterly. As a twenty-one year old, I started teaching my first Sunday School class—fifth-and sixth-grade boys. I had the privilege to lead several of those boys to faith in Christ. Two years later, I was moved to the College and Career Class. I taught there for about ten years. During this time, I coupled as the church Discipleship Training director and later became the church's Sunday School director. A few years following, the Lord was gracious to call me into the ministry of Christian Education.

Over the years as both a layman and a Minister of Education, I have developed the conviction that we need to get Sunday School back to the basics of the game and execute the fundamentals. It is my hope that this book will call us back to our core values. The discipline of executing these six fundamentals will result in a successful, fruitful Sunday School ministry. There is no magic involved in developing a healthy Sunday School - just hard work.

These six core values will manifest themselves in defining our ministry and directing our ministry. Individuals and organizations are both defined within the context of their core values. Others know you by what is important to you and lies within your inmost being.

Likewise, the two are directed and guided by that which they hold dear because your values are regarded as desirable and worthwhile. Like individuals, a ministry without core values will be easily sidetracked or altogether derailed. Our core values will shape us, for out of our principles come our philosophy and out of our philosophy comes our practices. Core values will help us move from doing things right to doing the right things. They will expose themselves in the litmus tests of setting standards, establishing policies, and making decisions.

Embracing these six core values will make your Sunday School manageable, measurable, and moveable!

CHAPTER 1

Sunday School Philosophy

Every church must decide what it will do with the Great Commission and how it will do it. The fact is, the Head of the Church, the Lord Jesus Christ, already has decided what we are to do:

> "And Jesus came and spake unto them, saying, All power is given unto me in heaven and in earth. Go ye therefore, and teach all nations, baptizing them in the name of the Father, and of the Son, and of the Holy Ghost: Teaching them to observe all things whatsoever I have commanded you: and, lo, I am with you alway, even unto the end of the world. Amen" (Matthew 28:18-20).

It is now up to us to determine how we should accomplish it.

Sunday School Vision Statement

To lead my local church to be a New Testament church by involving our people in the twofold mission of the Great Commission:

1. Evangelizing the unsaved.

2. Discipling the saved.

Every organization must have a vision or dream that gives it a purpose and mission. This vision gives direction and sets the agenda for the work of the organization. What then is the mission of the Sunday

School? Its number one purpose is to fulfill the Great Commission. The Sunday School is the church organized to do the work of the Great Commission. All other organizations within the church (discipleship training, choirs, etc.) recruit its people from those who are already part of the church fellowship. The Sunday School alone is the organization with the task of reaching people. Therefore, it is imperative the main objective for the Sunday School be reaching lost and unchurched people. We must have a heart for the Great Commission. If we do not, then not only will the Sunday School regress but so will

The Sunday School is the church organized

to do the work of the Great Commission.

the other organizations within the church which enlist those who have been brought in through the Sunday School ministry. Therefore, if the Sunday School does not reach people, then the whole church suffers.

When we lose sight of our purpose, then we become maintenance-driven instead of mission-driven. As someone has put it: "The main thing is to keep the main thing the main thing!"

How we view our Sunday School will have everything to do with what we do with it. I believe we need a new vision of what Sunday School is and what it can do. Sunday School is not just a program; it is a ministry. Sunday School is not just a weekly event; it is a strategy. You see, we would all agree that we are to be about the Great Commission. But the real issue is *how*. Sunday School is *how*. It is how we tangibly and practically flesh out the Great Commission. Question: If Sunday School is not how you flesh out the Great Commission, then how do we accomplish it? Is this method as effective as Sunday School? This I know, Sunday School has a track record that has been proven over the decades. Many say Sunday School is no longer effective and now fails us. My question is: Has Sunday School failed us, or have we failed Sunday School?

Sunday School Vision Strategy

The Sunday School Vision Strategy will answer the question how. How can we go about fulfilling the Great Commission? I see two crucial elements within the Sunday School structure that are musts if we are to effectively become more involved in the work of evangelizing and discipling. They are:

1. Developing New Leaders

2. Birthing New Units

If we have a vision statement which is the driving force behind a purpose-driven Sunday School, then we must have a strategy to bring this vision into a reality—the strategy being the small steps we must take in order to accomplish our predetermined goal. The two steps we must take are developing new leaders and birthing new units.

Step 1: Developing New Leaders

If the key to reaching new people is new units, then what is the key to birthing new units? Having new leaders! We must always be in the process of developing new leadership within the Sunday School organization. Groups created based on need alone will soon fizzle out. Genuine need must be coupled with genuine leadership for a new unit to survive. Leadership is the foundational support of any new unit. Everything rises and falls with leadership. Many new units which are birthed often are placed in an environment to fail instead of succeed because the leadership base was not in place. I strongly believe in birthing new units in order to grow, but I just as strongly believe the leaders must first be developed and in place.

Step 2: Birthing New Units

If the Sunday School is to continually reach lost and unchurched people, then we must be creating new units (new classes)—whether new classes or new care groups within those classes—to facilitate new people. New units grow faster than old ones. The old formula is still true: New Units = New People = New Growth.

Sunday School Vision Structure

The Sunday School must be structured to carry out the tasks of the organization. As mentioned in the *Sunday School Vision Statement,* the number one task of the organization is to reach lost and unchurched people. However, there are two other tasks the Sunday School should pursue. Therefore, the three tasks of Sunday School are:

1. Reach *people* for Christ and church membership.

2. Teach *people* God's Word.

3. Minister to *people's* needs.

Knowing our tasks, we can now set in place a leadership structure to support the objectives of the organization.

1. Teachers

Who will teach and be the leader for the class.

2. Outreach Leaders

Who will lead the class in reaching the lost and unchurched.

3. Care Group Leaders

Who will care for and pastor the people in their group.

Obviously, there are many other worthy endeavors which could be pursued within the organization. However, we unconsciously subvert the main things we need to do when we add additional tasks. Our tasks, like our *Vision Statement*, need to be short, to the point, and easily memorized to afford us the opportunity to know it by heart and center in on the bull's eye of the target. We need to know exactly what we are aiming for.

Our tasks need to be aligned with a leader who will be responsible for that task. Therefore, we will align our leaders with one of three tasks as follows:

Leader	*Task*
Teachers	Teach people God's Word.
Outreach Leaders	Reach people for Bible study.
Care Group Leaders	Minister to people's needs.

Each Sunday School class should have a Class Team consisting of a Teacher, Outreach Leader(s), and Care Group Leaders. The Outreach Leader(s) and Care Group Leaders will be accountable to the Teacher who will be accountable to their respective Division Director. All Teachers, Outreach Leaders, and Care Group Leaders become part of the Sunday School Leadership Team and are expected to meet at the Sunday School Leadership Meetings and at their Class Planning Meetings.

Each leader needs to know exactly what is expected of him in order to properly go about performing the functions of his responsibilities. So often we are disappointed in the efforts and performance of our leadership when, in fact, we have not given clear definition and explanation of the task.

Teacher

Responsibilities

1. To be responsible to lead the class to effectively reach, teach, and minister to people.

2. Conduct regular Class Planning Meetings with the Class Team.

3. Actively participate in the church's outreach program.

4. Prepare and present the Bible study lesson.

5. Be responsible to meet regularly with the Sunday School Leadership Team.

6. Lead the class to birth a new unit (class) each year.

7. Enlist an Associate Teacher and allow him/her to teach once a month for the purpose of developing a new teacher.

8. Conduct the Sunday morning class time in accordance with the "Class Time Structure" (see chapter eight on "Class Structure") so that the three purposes of the Sunday School can have a platform and proper emphasis.

The Call to Minister

My philosophy of a Sunday School class is: The class is a miniature congregation, and the teacher is a miniature pastor. Our thinking for this philosophy is: If a church is to grow, then the pastor must do certain things to enable it to grow: be actively reaching the unchurched, proclaiming God's Word, organizing the church for ministry, enlisting and equipping leaders, etc. Likewise, there are certain things a teacher must do to enable the class to grow: lead the group to reach people, share God's Word, organize the class for ministry, develop new leaders, etc. The teacher is, in fact, a "miniature minister" to that small group of people and does on a smaller scale what the pastor does on a larger scale. So the teacher's role is to be the leader for the class.

The class is a miniature congregation, and the teacher is a miniature pastor.

We have biblical instruction teaching us that all born-again believers are ministers—not just those who have been ordained. Jesus said, "...whosoever will be great among you, let him be your minister;...Even as the Son of man came not to be ministered unto, but to minister, and to give his life a ransom for many" (Matthew 20:26, 28). Therefore, the definition of a minister is someone who gives.

Many teachers have the idea: "I'll show up on Sunday morning, teach my class members for thirty minutes, go home, come back next week, and do it again." Our philosophy requires more of our teachers than a thirty-minute job once a week. It conveys the idea of ministry throughout the week and incorporating a team of leaders within the class to help conduct the ministry of the class.

Outreach Leader

Responsibilities

1. Participate weekly in the church's outreach program.

2. Lead the class to aggressively pursue lost and unchurched people.

3. Lead the class to discover prospects.

4. Be trained in the church's evangelism strategy.

5. Be a class Visitation Team Leader by enlisting two people from your class as your Visitation Team Learners each training semester.

6. Develop Visitation Team Learners from your class into Visitation Team Leaders.

7. Keep an updated prospect book.

8. Attend all Class Planning Meetings and Sunday School Leadership Meetings.

9. Lead the Sunday morning "Class Outreach Time" (see chapter eight on "Class Structure").

10. Serve as the class greeter and meet people as they enter the class each Sunday morning.

The Call to Evangelize

Too many outreach efforts are geared toward reaching the churched as opposed to reaching the unchurched. Our emphasis for outreach is to see lost people brought to a saving relationship with Jesus Christ. It is estimated that only fifteen percent of churches in America are growing. Of those fifteen percent, only one to three percent are actually growing through conversion growth; the others are growing by transfer growth. Most churches, therefore, are growing by "flock hop" which is sheep hopping from one flock to another. We need to put an emphasis on reaching and evangelizing LOST people.

Care Group Leader

Responsibilities

1. Be responsible to care and minister to approximately twelve people in your class.

2. Aggressively pursue delinquent members to restore them to the fellowship.

3. Attend all Class Planning Meetings and Sunday School Leadership Meetings.

4. Lead the Care Group time on Sunday morning by taking attendance, discovering ministry needs, involving others in meeting those needs, assigning contacts, and praying for each other (see chapter eight on "Class Structure").

5. Lead your Care Group to minister to the needs of those in your Care Group.

6. Lead the members of your Care Group to contact absentees on a weekly basis.

7. Involve the members of your Care Group to minister, contact, and care for others within your Care Group throughout the week.

8. Take attendance of your Care Group members each week, and coordinate the class roll with the class Secretary.

9. Actively participate in the church's outreach program.

The Call to Care

We have a good biblical concept of a shepherd since it is found so often in the Scriptures. As a good shepherd, these leaders handle pastoral care duties for the members of their Care Group and minister to their individual needs (death in the family, sickness, hospital stays, materialistic needs, etc.). A shepherd always stays with his flock of sheep and cares for their needs.

There are two other key players that will work in conjunction with the three main positions (Teacher, Outreach Leader, and Care Group Leaders). The first is a Class Administrator. He will become more necessary as the class grows larger. The teacher can do only so much and, as the class increases, so does the administration of the class.

Class Administrator

Responsibilities

1. Be responsible to the Teacher to organize and administrate the class.

2. Work with the Teacher in keeping the class on time and on task with the class time structure (see chapter eight on "Class Structure").

3. Discover, enlist, and equip class Outreach Leaders, Care Group Leaders, and Secretary.

4. Develop new leaders from the class's membership to place into service.

5. Attend all Class Planning Meetings and Sunday School Leadership Meetings.

6. Coordinate with the Teacher in planning and conducting the Class Planning Meeting.

7. Assist the Teacher in effectively reaching, teaching, and ministering to people.

8. Serve as shepherd and minister to the Care Group Leaders and Secretary.

9. Actively participate in the church's outreach program.

The Call to Organize

1 Corinthians 14:40 reads, "Let all things be done decently and in order." In Exodus 18, Jethro, Moses' father-in-law, helped him organize the Israelites so that effective ministry could take place. The Class Administrator will relieve the burden of many class administrative duties, so the Teacher can focus on teaching the Bible and leading the class in the three purposes of Sunday School.

Secretary

Responsibilities

1. Be responsible to oversee the class record-keeping system.

2. Work with the class Care Group Leaders in obtaining the class attendance.

3. Make sure all Visitor Forms have been properly filled out and turned in.

4. Inform the Class Administrator of all attending visitors, so they can be introduced and welcomed to the class.

5. Cooperate with the Class Administrator in assigning new members and visitors to a Care Group.

6. Make sure everyone wears a name tag on Sunday mornings.

7. Attend Class Planning Meetings and Sunday School Leadership Meetings.

The Call to Record

Several times in the Old Testament, God commanded the Israelites to take a census and count the people. Numbers are so important to God that He has dedicated one whole book in the Bible to "Numbers."

We believe in the old adage: "We count people because people count." Furthermore, we must have accurate records to make accurate decisions. My good friend and fellow staff member, Dan Dorner, has taught me: "Facts are our friends."

New Sunday School Mentality

Sunday School is more than an educational institution; it is a reaching, caring, ministering organization as well. Of our three tasks (1-Reach people for Bible study; 2-Teach people God's Word; 3-Minister to people's needs), only one has to do with education: teach. If only one-third of our tasks is educationally oriented, then we need to develop a new mentality toward the work and ministry of the Sunday School. Education is definitely part of what we do; and we will continue to put strong emphasis on the teaching of God's holy, inerrant Word. But education is not all we do. We also must have a mentality and vision that moves us to reach people for Christ and church membership. We cannot teach people God's Word if we first do not reach them. The Sunday School is better equipped to reach people than any other organization in the church. We are the biggest organization; we meet during "prime time" (Sunday morning); we are structured into age-graded units; and we are organized to quickly assimilate new people.

Sunday School is more than

an educational institution.

Then we must have the vision to minister to them. If God sends them to us, then surely He expects us to love and care for them. A Sunday School class should be a person's "spiritual support group." In fact, if a person does not get their needs met there, they will probably go unmet—we have no "Plan B."

Therefore, we must see Sunday School as something more than a one-hour happening on Sunday morning. This new vision will enable us to see it not as an event to attend once a week but as a ministry to embrace. The Sunday School is the church organized to carry out the Great Commission of our Lord Jesus Christ—which, by the way, is more than a Sunday morning event!

CORE VALUE
NUMBER ONE:

Reaching
People

CHAPTER 2

Why Outreach Should Be Done through Sunday School

The three tasks of Sunday School are: (1) reaching people, (2) teaching people, and (3) ministering to people. Of these three tasks, reaching people is the most important. Why? Because you can't teach those you don't reach and you can't minister as well to those you don't reach. Of the Six Core Values of Sunday School, reaching people has to be the most important one. Why? Because you don't assimilate people you don't reach; you don't involve people you don't reach; and you don't build strong, healthy relationships with people you don't reach. If you don't reach people, you can't even have Sunday School!

I once had the privilege and challenge of starting a "paper class." A "paper class" means you take no seed members from other classes; you simply list a number of prospects on a sheet of paper and then go after them. It took much hard work, a lot of visiting and phoning; but we were able to see that class grow, and many new people were united with the church and saved. I learned a valuable lesson: If no one was reached, we couldn't have Sunday School! Regardless of the hours I spent in study, if no one came, we could not teach. Regardless of the plans we made to assimilate people, involve them in ministry, build relationships with them, and put in place a great ministry, if no one came, if no one was reached, our plans would never become reality.

I read a story about a guy who woke up one morning in terrible pain. Every place he touched on his body enticed agony. He scratched his head, and it caused pain. He rubbed his shoulder, and the pain surfaced. He touched his knee, and pain shot throughout his body. He finally decided that something was terribly wrong with him, so he called the doctor's office to get an appointment. Even as he dialed the phone, the pain was unbearable. After consulting with the man, the doctor did a complete and thorough exam. As the doctor walked into the room to report his findings to the aching man, he frantically jumped up and asked the doctor if he was going to die. The doctor said, "No, according to the X-rays, you have a broken index finger."

A Sunday School devoid of evangelism is a broken index finger to the rest of the ministry of the church. It all starts with evangelism. No evangelism, no teaching, no discipleship, no involvement, no assimilation, no nothing! We must keep the main thing the main thing. As we plan and prioritize the work of the Sunday School, we must always keep evangelism on the front burner.

I am of the conviction that evangelism and outreach have to be promoted and emphasized more than any other of the Core Values because they do not take place on Sunday morning in the classroom. It easily falls into the syndrome of "out of sight, out of mind." Church leaders must talk about it and exemplify it.

Every Bible preaching/teaching church knows what we are to do: evangelize the unbeliever and disciple the believer. Again, Jesus Christ, the Head of the Church, has given us soldiers of the cross our marching orders: the Great Commission. So the question, "What are we to do?", is easily answered. I have found that the issue in the church is not *what* but *how*. *How* should we go about doing the what? We must build a strategy that is practical and intentional in its effort to fulfill the what. Sunday School is such a strategy! Sunday School is the best way to practically and tangibly flesh out the command of Christ upon our lives. Vision casting is done best in small groups; mobilization is best done in small groups. Therefore, the small group ministry is the best way to get our arms around the Great Commission.

Sunday School is the best way to practically and tangibly flesh out the command of Christ upon our lives.

As I have had the privilege to lead Sunday School conferences, I often conduct an exercise where the conferees list the purposes of the Sunday School in the order of priority. Overwhelmingly, Bible study is listed as the number one purpose of Sunday School. Ministering to one another, fellowshipping with one another, and praying for one another are the other priorities given. No one could argue against these things. They are very important and should be a vital part of any Sunday School class. But we seem to always place the highest priority on what we do "with one another." Again, let me reaffirm their necessity. I would not want to be a part of a Sunday School that did not cherish these things. However, I am compelled to ask this insightful question: If Jesus Christ was still incarnate and here on earth and was your Sunday School teacher, what would be His number one priority for His class? I believe we find our answer from the Lord Jesus Christ Himself.

- "For the Son of man is come to seek and to save that which was lost" (Luke 19:10).

- "...I am come that they might have life, and that they might have it more abundantly" (John 10:10).

- "For God sent not his Son into the world to condemn the world; but that the world through him might be saved" (John 3:17).

- "...for I came not to judge the world, but to save the world" (John 12:47).

- "And when his disciples James and John saw this, they said, Lord, wilt thou that we command fire to come down from heaven, and consume them, even as Elijah did? But he turned, and rebuked them, and said, Ye know not what manner of spirit ye are of. For the Son of man is not come to destroy men's lives, but to save them..." (Luke 9:54-56).

I think Scripture is clear. If Jesus Christ were your Sunday School teacher, He would lead the class to be evangelistically driven. I have often asked myself this question: "If Jesus Christ was the Minister of Education at First Baptist Church, Woodstock, Georgia, what would He lead the Sunday School to do?" When I ask myself that question, I find my purpose for our Sunday School ministry. With these thoughts in mind, let me give you five reasons evangelism should be done through the Sunday School.

If Jesus Christ were your Sunday School teacher, He would lead the class to be evangelistically driven.

1. Sunday School is the church organized to carry out the Great Commission.

In most churches, the Sunday School is the ministry that is mandated with the task to reach people. The discipleship program is not designed to reach lost and unchurched people; it is designed to mature the people who have already received Christ and who are in the church. The choir is not mandated with the task of reaching people; it is mandated with the purpose of ushering the people who have already been reached into the presence of God during the time of corporate worship. Our committees are not charged with the task of reaching people. As one old sage put it: "For God so loved the world that He didn't send a committee!" Our committees are responsible to oversee some aspect of the church. You see, it is our Sunday School that shoulders the objective of evangelizing and reaching the lost. And if the Sunday School doesn't do it, then pray tell, who will? Answer: Nobody! And that's precisely what's happening in churches all across America. We are reaching no one because we do not have a how strategy!

Every year it is typical for 10,000 churches in our Southern Baptist Convention to not baptize one person. Can you imagine that? Not even one little boy or girl in a year's time that was led to saving faith in Christ! If each one of those churches had just four Sunday School classes – one preschool class, one children's class, one youth class, and one adult class – that would be 40,000 classes that saw no one saved. That's 40,000 Sunday School teachers that led no one to salvation. Do we teachers only teach people to fish, or should we be fishermen ourselves? That's 40,000 Sunday School classes that put no how behind their what. God forgive us! God help us!

2. Sunday School is the largest ministry in the church.

In the average church, Sunday School is the largest ministry in the church. Therefore, it stands to reason that the biggest ministry in the church should be responsible for the biggest priority of the church. I have a friend that attends a church that averages about 200 people each week. At their church, the task of evangelism and outreach is relegated to an "Evangelism Committee" comprised of six people. Why would a church whittle down the number of people carrying out the task of evangelism and outreach? Obviously, they have a low priority for this all-important task. I would attempt to mobilize all 200. I understand that all of them would not involve themselves as soul winners, but surely they could involve more than six!

3. Sunday School has groups that are…

• Small.

This makes it easier to know people and build relationships. It also places the prospect in an environment where they can share, ask questions, and have their needs met.

• Age-graded.

This allows us to reach people by those who have similar lifestyles. Being connected to a homogeneous group makes it easier to share with the unchurched, reach the unchurched, and assimilate the unchurched once they do attend. Your evangelism strategy should never be divorced from your assimilation strategy! Evangelism and discipleship are not separate but two parts to the same process. Therefore, to alienate your assimilation strategy from your evangelism strategy is to abort the Great Commission process in a person's life. Sunday School is uniquely structured to reach and to assimilate.

4. Sunday School meets during "prime time."

Sunday School meets on Sunday morning or during "prime time." Since most people attend church on Sunday mornings, then it stands

Sunday School is uniquely structured to reach and to assimilate.

to reason that you would want your Sunday morning ministry to undertake the task of reaching and assimilating people. Again, your reaching ministry must be connected to your assimilation ministry! It is generally true that what reaches them keeps them. Sunday School is the "prime time" ministry of a local church and should be respected for that and structured for that.

5. Our Bible studies will...

• Lead attending lost people to faith in Christ.

The Bible IS God speaking to us. If the Word of God will not lead someone to Christ, then we have no hope of seeing anyone repent and trust the death, burial, and resurrection of Christ for their salvation.

• "For the word of God is quick, and powerful, and sharper than any twoedged sword, piercing even to the dividing asunder of soul and spirit, and of the joints and marrow, and is a discerner of the thoughts and intents of the heart" (Hebrews 4:12).

Our Bible studies will point men, women, boys, and girls to Jesus. Jesus said, "And I, if I be lifted up from the earth, will draw all men unto me" (John 12:32). The Word of God does just that – it lifts up the Son of God! I have a strong confidence in the Word of God; I have placed my life upon it. In fact, I have placed my eternal life upon the integrity and power of the Word of God! I believe people will come to Jesus as we teach the infallible, inerrant Word of God.

• "Search the scriptures; for in them ye think ye have eternal life: and they are they which testify of me" (John 5:39).

Sunday School is a place where people can and should be saved. It is recommended that teachers occasionally offer a gospel invitation at the close of the Bible study. This invitation does not have to be like the one a pastor might offer at the close of the worship service, but we must understand that people can and will be saved if the Word of God has been presented.

Sunday School is a place where people can and should be saved.

- "So then faith cometh by hearing, and hearing by the word of God" (Romans 10:17).

Now this verse is true or it is not. I emphasize again that the Word of God will do its perfect work in the hearts of people. The prophet Isaiah instructed us well in this thought:

- "So shall my word be that goeth forth out of my mouth: it shall not return unto me void, but it shall accomplish that which I please, and it shall prosper in the thing whereto I sent it" (Isaiah 55:11).

- Motivate our people to have a passion for the lost.

You cannot study the Bible and not see God's heart for people. The Bible clearly shows God's continuous activity to redeem fallen mankind. A serious, conscientious study of Scripture will produce a passion to become a soul winner.

A serious, conscientious study of Scripture will produce a passion to become a soul winner.

There has been much talk in the last ten to fifteen years that you can no longer go door to door and you can no longer confront people with the gospel. I want to go on record to say: "It ain't so." Now I realize some communities have security gates and will not let you enter. But there are still many places one can go, and there are still hundreds of people we rub elbows with every day. I am afraid that we have just about talked ourselves out of being witnesses of the gospel of the grace of God. The Apostle Paul, however, was bold in presenting the gospel:

- "For I am not ashamed of the gospel of Christ: for it is the power of God unto salvation to every one that believeth..." (Romans 1:16).

- "Knowing therefore the terror of the Lord, we persuade men..." (2 Corinthians 5:11).

- "And he (Paul) reasoned in the synagogue every sabbath, and persuaded the Jews and the Greeks" (Acts 18:4).

- And he (Paul) went into the synagogue, and spake boldly for the space of three months, disputing and persuading the things concerning the kingdom of God" (Acts 19:8).

I find no scriptural admonition to be timid with the gospel or our witness. In fact, the very opposite is encouraged:

- "And for me, that utterance may be given unto me, that I may open my mouth *boldly*, to make known the mystery of the gospel. For which I am an ambassador in bonds: that therein I may speak *boldly, as I ought to speak*" (Ephesians 6:19-20, *emphasis mine*).

CHAPTER 3

Ten Observations for Effective Outreach through Sunday School

There are many issues that can make a Sunday School more effective in reaching people. It is clear all of the Core Values contribute to the effectiveness and productivity of the others. I want to present ten observations that will help your Sunday School become more effective in outreach. This list is not intended to be exhaustive. These observations are presented with the hope of being somewhat useful.

1. Effective outreach will not develop without the intentional efforts and emphasis by church leaders.

Like anything else in life, little is accomplished if we don't get intentional about it. I am currently doing some maintenance and repairs on my house. I have put these projects off for as long as I can. I have not seen to these before because I was not intentional. My wife is now helping me get intentional! Church work is no different than home work. It takes an intentionality to the tasks at hand. When it comes to evangelism and outreach, there are three intentional areas that must receive attention by the church leadership.

A. Personnel

There must be people appointed to lead the outreach efforts of the Sunday School. If a job is to be done, then someone has to "own" the task. As long as any objective of the church remains the job of everybody, then nobody will see to it. Nothing becomes dynamic until it becomes specific! We can no longer afford for evangelism to remain in the domain of generality. Therefore, each class must have a person(s) assigned with the specific responsibility of overseeing the outreach endeavors of the class.

As long as any objective of the church remains the job of everybody, then nobody will see to it. Nothing becomes dynamic until it becomes specific!

When our children were younger, my wife Linda would cook a big breakfast on Saturday mornings and we would enjoy each other's fellowship over the breakfast table. Then we would divide chores among our three children and get busy cleaning the house. I noticed if we never specifically assigned a certain chore to be done, then it remained undone.

When I go to McDonald's for lunch, I notice everyone there has specific jobs to do. The manager doesn't say to the employees as they arrive for work: "Many hungry people will come here today, so everyone just jump in and help out where you can." That would be a disaster! The manager at McDonald's makes sure every task is specifically seen to and "owned" by an employee.

Why is it that McDonald's is wiser than the church? We need not expect things to get done if no one is assigned to specific tasks. This is especially true of evangelism and outreach. Why? Because (1) evangelism and outreach take place outside of the Sunday experience and (2) the devil fights against them with all he has. He is ambitious, and he wants every soul he can possibly deceive. I have learned that the two things Satan fights against the most in my life are my personal quiet time with the Lord and my participation in soul winning.

Let me share what I perceive as being important in the church:

• Preaching – that is why we designate a person as the preacher.

• Bible study – that is why we designate people as teachers.

• Prayer – that is why we designate people as prayer warriors.

• Fellowship – that is why we designate a "Fellowship Leader" or church hostess.

• Music – that is why we designate a person to lead the music and choirs to sing.

• Ministry – that is why we designate deacons.

• Offering – that is why we designate ushers to receive it.

• Buildings – that is why we designate persons to be on the Building and Grounds Committee.

The obvious question: Why do we not designate persons in our Sunday School to oversee the church's outreach ministry?

B. Schedule

There must be a designated time that is regularly scheduled for ongoing outreach. Some would say we should just witness "as we go."

I agree. However, I do not want to make an "either/or" out of outreach; I want it to be a "both/and." Let's witness as we go, and let's witness at a designated time.

May I again share what I perceive as being important in the church:

- Preaching – that is why we designate a time for it.

- Bible study – that is why we designate a time for Sunday School.

- Prayer – that is why we designate a time for Prayer Meeting.

- Fellowship – that is why we designate certain dates and times for church socials and gatherings.

- Music – that is why we designate a time for choir practice.

- Ministry – that is why we designate persons to do hospital visits.

- Offering – that is why we designate a time in the worship service to receive it.

- Buildings – that is why we designate a meeting time for the Building and Grounds Committee.

The obvious question: Should we not designate a time for the thing that is nearest and dearest to God's heart—soul winning? To me, it is hypocritical to say we ought to designate a time for all these things that are vitally important to a church and then leave out a time designated specifically for evangelism. Why, we wouldn't dare think of doing away with the time to:

- Receive tithes and offerings by suggesting people do that "as they go."

Should we not designate a time for
the thing that is nearest and dearest
to God's heart—soul winning?

- Worship corporately by suggesting people do that "as they go."

- Study the Bible by suggesting people do that "as they go."

- Have choir practice by suggesting people do that "as they go."

C. Budget

There must be monies budgeted for the purpose of supporting the Sunday School's outreach program. It's time we "put our money where our mouth is." We talk a good game of evangelism but often fail to play a good game. Churches should evaluate their budget to see if they are supporting evangelistic efforts with the needed dollars.

As individuals, we spend our money on what's important to us. So it is with a church. The church budget will reflect the priorities of the church. We budget money to supply a free meal and childcare to anyone participating in our church's outreach program on visitation nights. It is not inexpensive to do this, but then just how much is a soul worth? Jesus said it was worth more than the whole world. (Matthew 16:26) What does your church need: more stuff or more souls?

How a church employs her personnel,
schedule, and budget makes a statement
as to what is important to the church.

How a church employs her personnel, schedule, and budget makes a statement as to what is important to the church. What's important in your church?

2. Those who visit the church are the greatest prospects for church membership.

This is a "no-brainer" statement, but I do not want us to miss it. Sometimes we get so involved in discovering new prospects that we forget about the ones right under our nose. Each week at visitation, we make sure we visit the "hot prospects" before we distribute any other visits. The "hot prospects" are the ones who visited our worship service or Sunday School the week before.

Let me illustrate by again taking you to McDonald's (I'm getting hungry). When I go there and order a number-one combo meal, I always know what is coming next. You see, McDonald's has trained their employees well. Every time I order the number-one combo meal, the next words I hear are: "Would you like to super-size that?" To which I always respond, "Yes." I know a deal when I see one. Where else could I go to get that many extra fat grams for 39 cents! But here is the lesson from McDonald's: They understand the greater chance of selling me more food than the guy driving down the street because I am in the restaurant. I am, in fact, a "hot prospect" for McDonald's because I am in their building.

When a person visits your church and/or Sunday School, they are a "hot prospect." The fact they would attend says they at least have some interest in the church and spiritual things or else they would not have attended in the first place. Therefore, these people are "hot prospects" and should be followed up immediately while they still retain some interest. We need to visit these people the following week and see if we can "super size" them.

When we send our people out to visit, they go with a twofold purpose. The first is to share the gospel and attempt to bring people into a personal relationship with the Lord Jesus Christ. The second purpose is to enroll them in Sunday School. We practice open enrollment which means we will enlist anyone in Sunday School at anytime and in any place. A person has to be saved to be a church member, but they do not have to be saved to be a Sunday School member. I have often said we have only one qualification for people to be Sunday School members – they must have a pulse! We want to place lost and unchurched people in an environment conducive for the Spirit's work in their lives. Sunday School is such an environment. It places the unbeliever with God's people and in God's Word. This makes for fertile soil where the seed of faith can germinate.

3. Most unchurched people attend church because of the relationship they have with a friend or family member.

As a general rule, people attend church where they know someone. Relationships build the bridge to the church for the unchurched person. I do not frequent bars because (1) I do not adhere to that way of life and (2) I do not have relationships with many who do. The same is true for the unbeliever. He does not attend church because (1) he does not hold to the same doctrines of life and (2) he does not hang out with believers. So how is the church going to reach him? Certainly, we must depend on the work of the Holy Spirit in his life. But we also must attempt to witness to him, care for him, and build a relationship with him. Relationships build trust. As the unbeliever

Relationships build the bridge to
the church for the unchurched person.

grows to trust a Christian and builds a relationship with him, the believer is building a bridge to the church and to Christ.

   4. Prospects should be visited and cultivated by those of their
      potential Sunday School class.

Prospects should be assigned to the Sunday School class where they would go if they came. The thirty-year-old class should not be visiting the sixty-year-old couple. This is better than no visit at all, but it certainly is not the ideal. Remember, your evangelism/outreach efforts should be directly tied to your discipleship/assimilation strategy. The sixty-year-old class then should visit the sixty-year-old couple, and the thirty-year-old class should visit the thirty-year-old folks. This necessitates every class being represented each week at visitation.

> *Your evangelism/outreach efforts*
> *should be directly tied to your*
> *discipleship/assimilation strategy.*

Because of Observations 3 and 4, prospects should be visited on a consistent basis by the same visitation team and not passed around among several people because...

A. No relationship can be cultivated.

If a different member of the class visits an unchurched family every visit, then we make it difficult to build a relationship and form a bond with the family. If different visitation teams are used to visit a prospect, then it cripples the ability to build the all-important relationship. It becomes, in effect, a "hit and run" proposition each week.

Again, this is better than not visiting at all; but it is not the optimum.

B. No member is "owning" the prospect for Jesus.

At some point, we have to take ownership of people and be committed to work with them, build relationships with them, and witness to them. A salesman would not pass his potential buyers to another salesman and miss his commission. Companies know many people buy their product because of the relationship they have developed with their customers. Likewise, we need to develop trusting relationships with people, earn their trust, and have the opportunity to see them come to faith in Christ.

Occasionally, one of our visitation teams will return from a visit, hand me the visitation assignment card, and say, "This is a great prospect and needs follow up." I always respond by handing them the assignment card back and saying, "Then follow up. You've met these people; you know where they live; you know something about them and have even made friends with their dog. So follow up." They have begun the relationship-building process, so why would I send out another team in a week or two who would have to start from scratch? I want each team to "own" some folks for Christ's sake.

5. Approximately fifty percent of outreach efforts should be consumed in *discovering* and *qualifying* prospects. The other fifty percent of outreach efforts should be used in pursuing the identified and qualified prospects.

Please grab hold of this principle without getting hung up on the percentage amounts. Some churches may spend sixty percent of their outreach manhours discovering and qualifying prospects and the other forty percent pursuing the identified and qualified prospects. The exact percentage will vary from church to church. The principle is vital to understand because you want to be a good steward of the time people invest in outreach. Time is a limited resource and must be used wisely. When people come to visit, you want to make sure they fish in a pond with real, live fish—visiting persons who are lost, or unchurched, and genuine prospects.

Let's say a dedicated Christian lady visits your church to support her twelve-year-old niece who is being baptized. This lady faithfully attends another church in the community. She is happy there and very involved in the ministries of her church. This lady is not a prospect for your church. If she is assigned to a visitation team, then they will have sweet fellowship with her on the visit but will be ineffective in reaching the lost and unchurched. A little time spent qualifying this person as a prospect would have saved the valuable time of those who made that visit. We try to qualify our prospects by getting the following information from them:

- Name, address, phone number, and email address. If you don't have this information, then you don't have a prospect.

- Birthday. This helps us know which Sunday School class should receive the visitation assignment.

Then we ask these questions:

- Do you attend church as often as once a month?

- If so, where? (If they attend as often as once a month and they can name the church, then they are not a prospect for our church.)

- If you were to die today, are you certain you would have eternal life with God in heaven? (They can respond in three ways: "Yes," "No," or "Not Sure." If they check "No" or "Not Sure," then they are prospects—regardless if they attend church once a month or not.)

This is not a perfect system, but it does help us to be good stewards of the time our people invest in our outreach/visitation program.

6.   Use people where they are usable.

The church needs to use people where they are and then try to develop them in their spiritual pilgrimage and service. A great principle in church work is this: The secret to success is the involvement of people. Therefore, plug people in where you can. Some people are not comfortable knocking on a door and sharing their faith. Do I think they ought to do this? Yes. However, I must accept people where they are, use them where they are, but do not leave them where they are. This means I must have other means for people to involve themselves in the outreach ministry of the church. Many reach out through avenues of benevolence. They carry food to those in need; they feed the homeless; they provide clothes for the poor. A church clothes closet and food pantry can touch many unsaved people. In addition, allow people to make phone calls or write cards. These touches also serve as a valuable way to let prospects know we care.

I once heard a preacher say he was burdened about a man that was lost. His wife was a faithful member of the church and a precious saint of God. So the preacher visited the lost man one night, shared the gospel with him, and then pleaded with the man to come to Christ. But the man would not receive Christ. A week or two later, the lost man attended worship with his godly wife. The pastor preached his sermon and then offered the invitation. The congregation stood, and the choir sang "Just As I Am." The lost man stepped into the aisle and made his way to the preacher. The preacher was so excited he could hardly contain himself. The lost man took the preacher's hand and said, "Preacher, I'd like to ask you a question." The preacher's heart was about to beat out of his chest as he knew the man was going to ask how he could be saved. The preacher shook his hand; and the man asked, "Pastor, have you ever bungee jumped?" The pastor was flabbergasted and didn't know how to respond to such a question. This was a solemn and serious moment. The choir was singing "Just As I Am"; a plea had been made to come to Christ; and this man walks the aisle to ask such a question! Since the preacher didn't know what to do, he went along with this man and answered his question: "No, I have never bungee jumped in my life." The lost man then asked another question: "Pastor, did you ever jump off the high dive at the swimming pool?" The pastor is now getting more anxious, wondering where this conversation is going, but politely answers, "Yes." Then the lost man asked one more question: "Pastor, before you jumped off the high dive at the swimming pool, did you first jump off the low dive to sort of acclimate yourself?" "Well, yes," the pastor replied. Then the man said, "Pastor, I appreciate you coming to the house the other night to talk with me. But I felt like you were asking me to bungee jump into heaven when I haven't been off the low dive or the high dive yet."

He needed to be cultivated some more. He needed to be processed more. He just wasn't ready yet. Now let's turn that story and put a different twist on it. When it comes to knocking on a door and sharing a plan of salvation, many Christians see that as a bungee jump into soul winning and they are not ready yet. What should we do then? Discard them as second-rate believers? No, let's take them where they are and grow them to where they need to be. Let's put some of them on the high dive, and let them make phone calls. Let's put the rest of them on the low dive, and have them write cards and letters. But by all means, let's put ALL of the saints to work and involve them in the priority of the church – reaching people!

7. Special events can be a great outreach tool if prospects are registered, visited, cultivated, and assimilated quickly.

Does your church do events, or do you have events with a purpose? It is great to expose people to the church through Christmas pageants, Halloween alternatives, sports programs, Vacation Bible School, etc.; but use these events beyond the event. Make sure everyone is registered, so you can follow up on them. If they attend a special event at your church, you need to see if you can "super size" them.

You can encourage people to register (name, address, phone number, email address, birthday, etc.) by giving away door prizes. Everyone who registers becomes a candidate to win. Then you make sure the only cards used for the drawing are guests. Let them win. Let them have an enjoyable experience at the church. If you give away umbrellas, make sure they have the church's name and logo on it. Every time it rains, they will be reminded of your church and the good experience they had there. This gives the church good "hang time" with the prospect.

8. New members should be assimilated quickly; they have many unchurched friends to bring with them.

New people have a circle of influence from which to draw. The most excited people in your church are your new members. If they were not excited, they would have joined another church. Tap into the new member's realm of influence by having them fill out cards on people they know who need a church home. Also tap into their excitement for the church, and have them join a visitation team that visits these people.

New Christians are another good source to accumulate prospects for the church. Unbelievers, as a general rule, do not run around with believers. They can be a great source of prospecting, and you can immediately teach them how to be a soul winner by involving them with a team to reach their lost friends and acquaintances.

9. Getting people zealous about outreach is rarely a "quick fix" proposition; it is a long-term process, requiring perseverance and focus.

Winston Churchill said, "The nose of a bulldog is slanted backwards, so he can continue to breath without turning loose." When it comes to evangelism and outreach, we must be more than dogmatic; we must be "bulldogmatic!" We must grab hold of the Great Commission and not turn loose for anything.

When it comes to evangelism and outreach,
we must be more than dogmatic;
we must be "bulldogmatic!"

You may read this and get all fired up about reaching people and mobilizing the Sunday School for evangelism. You may stand before your Sunday School class and give a rousing evangelistic challenge— only to find that very few share your zeal. But don't quit. Be bull-dogmatic. You need to understand that building an evangelistic Sunday School will take time. It is a process, requiring years of continual emphasis and work.

I have found the best way to enlist people for outreach is to employ the "button-hole enlistment strategy." This one-on-one approach is when you talk to a person individually about his or her call to become a Great Commission Christian.

I had an experience like this with a Sunday School teacher. Mike was a great student of the Word of God and a wonderful teacher but never came to weekly visitation. One Sunday, I spoke with him privately and asked him why he never came to outreach on Monday night. He was very honest in expressing his fear of knocking on the door of someone he did not know. I told him he could be my partner, and I would do all the talking; then he could be praying while I was sharing. I asked him if he could pray; and he said he could—or he would have appeared to be unspiritual. So I said to him: "Good, I'll see you tomorrow night at 6:30." I then turned away and did not give him a chance to respond.

Sure enough, the next evening rolled around and here came Mike. We went visiting and had a great time together. As we returned to the church, I told Mike we would do this again next week and I looked forward to seeing him then.

He came the second week, and we had the glorious opportunity to lead a single mom to the Lord. She got down on her knees, wept before the Lord, and invited Jesus Christ to come into her life! As we were pulling out of the apartment complex, Mike was ecstatic. He said, "I have never seen anything like this before!" I asked, "Mike, have you never seen anyone get saved?" "Sure I have, Allan, but not like that. I've only witnessed people being saved at church," he said. Mike went on to say, "I have never seen anyone witnessed to in their home and then get on their knees, repent of their sins, and receive Jesus." Well, needless to say, from that day forward, I couldn't get a word in edgewise. Mike wanted to do all the witnessing, while I did all the praying!

Six months later, I suggested to Mike that we each now take another person and train them. We both loved the fellowship that we had but knew the cause of the kingdom made this move necessary. So we both "button-holed" a trainee, and off we went again. At the start of the year, I was involved in the church's evangelistic efforts. By the end of the year, there were four of us.

You must understand that building a soul-winning army will take time, perseverance, and focus. Don't lose heart, dear friend. Press on!

10. All of the planning in the world will not replace an aggressive, obedient spirit to "go out into the highways and hedges, and compel them to come in, that my house may be filled" (Luke 14:23).

We have tried to find ways, methods, and yes, even tricks to encourage evangelism. The truth of the matter is that we need people with a heart for others. We need people with a heart like that of God who would send His only begotten Son for the likes of me. We need people to have the heart of Jesus who laid down His life so that we might have life and the assurance of heaven. All of the programs and methods in the world will be rendered useless and ineffective if we do not have people who will be obedient to the call to "Go."

> *All of the programs and methods in the*
> *world will be rendered useless and*
> *ineffective if we do not have people*
> *who will be obedient to the call to "Go."*

When it comes to evangelism, it is better to err on the side of aggressiveness than on the side of passiveness. People are dying and going to hell. At the rate we are losing the world, it is safe to say we have erred on the side of being too timid. In our efforts to not offend anyone, we have lost the much needed boldness to share Christ. As I once heard Dr. Adrian Rogers say, "Where are we going to scare the lost to? Hell number two?"

Peter was identified as a follower of Christ on the night he denied the Lord three times because "thy speech betrayeth thee" (Matthew 26:73). I was raised in East Tennessee, and my "speech betrayeth me" as well. But let me use a little East Tennessee hillbilly twang to make a point about being aggressive in pursuing the call to "Go":

Ain't hardly nobody been saved what ain't been went after!

CORE VALUE
NUMBER TWO:

Teaching
People

CHAPTER 4

Teacher Enlistment

The most important thing we do to build a strong Sunday School is enlist teachers. Teachers are the Most Valuable Players of your Sunday School. To have a good Sunday School is to have good teachers. Conversely, to have bad teachers is to have a bad Sunday School. You cannot build a great organization without great people. Therefore, the importance of proper enlistment of teachers cannot be overstated. As we mentioned in chapter one, teachers are to the class what the pastor is to the church. The teacher is, in fact, a "miniature pastor"; and his class is his "miniature congregation." The teacher must feed them and lead them in the way they are to go.

To have a good Sunday School is to have good teachers.

The owner of a car dealership will do all he can to put good salesmen on his car lot. Good salesmen make for good sales. The owner knows his success, or lack thereof, lies in the men or women on the lot making contact with customers. So it is in Sunday School. The success, or lack thereof, will be the result of our teachers.

The proper enlistment of teachers then becomes a vital link in placing our Sunday School in a successful environment. I want to walk you through an eight-step process of "Sunday School Enlistment Principles." These simple steps will aid you in enlisting teachers and, with a few adjustments, also can be used to enlist other workers as well.

Explore the Possibilities

It is apparent you cannot enlist those who you know nothing about. You must have a way to get information on prospective teachers. There are many ways to do this, but I like to get a recommendation from their current Sunday School teacher. Their teacher has been able to observe them over a period of time. The teacher can see the spiritual growth in this person's life. The teacher is aware of their faithfulness to attend class, church services, outreach opportunities, service to others, etc. The teacher is in a position to know more about this person than most anyone else. It could be a Care Group Leader also would have some insight into this person's walk with God and dedication to the local church.

Unless there are some unusual circumstances, I would not recommend enlisting those who have been unfaithful to attend Sunday School. A person devoid of class attendance is usually a person devoid of personal spiritual growth. It has been my observation through the years that the people who love the Word and want to learn more of it are in Sunday School. There is a leadership question at stake as well: How can a person be a good leader if he has not first been a good follower? It is easy to be persuaded to make exceptions for those who are well liked and charismatic. Again, my experience tells me there is a trouble spot waiting in the road ahead if you make this your practice.

Engage the Process

After receiving the recommendation from the prospect's current class leadership, I like to meet with the person one on one. I will set up an appointment and meet with the prospect face to face. I do not want to talk about this important issue of teaching Sunday School over the phone or as I can grab a person between Sunday School and church service. I want a dedicated time to sit down with the prospect and dialogue with him. I want to get to know him as a person and as a Christian. I want him to tell me his life story and his testimony. At this time, I want to join the person in prayer and commit to pray for him as he continues to seek God's will in this matter. I will offer no formal invitation at this time.

Expectations Presented

During this one-on-one meeting, I will share the expectations we have for our Sunday School teachers. It may be your Sunday School Council, pastor, and/or other entities in your church establish what expectations will be required of your teachers. It is essential that the proper authorities are involved because there will be challenges to this process at some point and the church needs to be unified in her approach.

We share our expectations by handing the prospect several documents and discussing them at this face-to-face meeting. The first document is our *Sunday School Philosophy*. Chapter one of this book represents this document. We want the prospect to know what we are about and why we do it. We want them to understand the concept of our ministry and how we structure our ministry to accomplish the three tasks of Sunday School. Therefore, we spend time discussing this document with the prospect.

Secondly, we explain our *Sunday School Covenant* (see Appendix 1). We expect commitment from our teachers; and this is the tool we use to define it and then have them sign it, indicating their commitment to these items. This document has weeded many out of teaching Sunday School. It is gut wrenching to lose a potential teacher but less painful than putting up with a bad one. Our approach is to establish commitment up front so that we avoid the unpleasant situation of confronting indifference later on. We really do enlist about ninety-five percent of our problems. If we will enlist workers properly, it will save many headaches in the future.

I take the *Sunday School Covenant* and talk the prospect through each of the twelve issues. Here they are—along with some of my commentary to the prospect.

1. I have a personal relationship with God through Jesus Christ.

It doesn't get any more basic than this, but this is the most critical issue. I operate under the premise you should never take anything for granted—especially in this day and age. I have jokingly but truly stated that a saved Sunday School teacher makes a better teacher! Amen! You will see later we have them fill out the form *My Personal Testimony* which also helps in knowing their personal encounter with our resurrected Lord.

2. I feel called of God to serve Him through the Sunday School.

I want people serving in our Sunday School ministry who feel called of God to do so. I have suffered through the agony of dealing with Nominating Committees who were more interested in "filling slots" than finding God-called people to serve. I want to defend Nominating Committees because the way we have established them and set them up has lent itself to "slot filling." It is my conviction that each ministry leader should enlist their own workers. No one knows the ministry like those who live it and are called to it. Furthermore, I believe the person to whom you answer is the person who should be enlisting you.

3. I will strive to follow the leadership of the Holy Spirit.

Every class and every individual has their own makeup and special needs. Therefore, I want people walking in the Spirit to be leading our people. If we want our pastor to be a Spirit-filled man, then we should have the same desire for our "miniature pastors."

4. I will actively participate in training and growing opportunities.

It is unfathomable for a teacher to enter service trained and well equipped only to have him become stagnant in the years to come to the point that he is not making the impact he should. I would rather sit under a teacher who is "green" but growing than to sit under one who is mature but stagnant. I don't want a teacher who always relies on yesterday's knowledge. I want one who is sprouting, growing, maturing, and becoming.

We offer monthly training, two training events a year, and a personal annual evaluation that enable us to keep growth opportunities before our Sunday School leaders and any potential leaders. Training is one of the things to which we are committed, and this commitment is reflected in our calendar and in our budget. If a prospect is unwilling to progressively grow, then they will be incapable of reaching their God-given potential. It is a tragedy to waste the gifts and abilities God has placed within you that you allow to remain dormant.

Training is one of the things to which we are committed, and this commitment is reflected in our calendar and in our budget.

5. I will actively participate in reaching lost and unchurched persons.

If our number-one purpose for Sunday School is to reach people, then it stands to reason that our teachers (miniature pastors) need to be involved in reaching the unchurched and witnessing to the lost. The teacher's example in this area is crucial in influencing class members to go into "the highways and hedges and compel them."

It often becomes difficult for teachers to study several hours during the week, attend Wednesday night activities, and give a night for visitation. This is especially true of moms who have children and/or work outside the home. However, we do ask our teachers to be systematically and regularly involved in our visitation program. A teacher must teach, but a teacher also must lead. Again, I illustrate this by using the pastor. He must preach, but he must lead the church as well. The leadership provided by the teacher in evangelism and soul winning is paramount to its success!

The leadership provided by the teacher
in evangelism and soul winning
is paramount to its success!

6. I will actively participate in Sunday School leadership meetings.

We expect our teachers to attend our Sunday School leadership meetings on the third Sunday of each month since it is the Sunday least affected by holidays. Our meetings start at 4:00 P.M. and are finished in time to attend the 6:00 P.M. worship service.

I am amazed at the churches that do not hold these valuable meetings. When I coached high school football, I would not even entertain the idea that some of my players would miss practice. They were expected to be there, and only sickness or a family death would excuse them. We could not expect to win on Friday night if we had not properly prepared during the week.

We would think it ridiculous if the choir never practiced yet wanted to sing on Sunday morning. But yet we think we can get by without our Sunday School leaders coming together for planning and preparation. Maybe that's what we are doing – just getting by! We are barely surviving but not thriving. This is a shame to God who gave everything for us! The rule at our church is that no one sings in the choir if they cannot come to choir practice, AND no one teaches Sunday School if they cannot attend our leadership meetings.

7. I will do all I can to make Sunday mornings a positive, uplifting experience.

The most uplifting things in the world are God's salvation, God's Word, and God's people. I want teachers who are positive, loving, and friendly people. People don't follow negative leadership. It is shameful to the church that people have to go to a bar to experience "happy hour." I believe the happiest hour of the week in a person's life is the hour they spend in Sunday School!

I don't get excited about some disgruntled Christian who is teaching Sunday School. He takes a "sin of the week" and badgers everyone with it. Now I am not a proponent of skirting issues nor do I want my teachers to avoid addressing sin, calling it what it is and exposing its destructive ramifications. But I do want them to show people how to live godly, how to avoid Satan's deathly traps, and how to live victoriously and experience the abundant life. I want our people leaving Sunday School with hope that they can live godly in Christ Jesus and not feel defeated by some warped teacher who feels it is his duty to beat people up.

I like for the teacher to be there early, shaking hands and interacting with his class members. He should set the tone and atmosphere of the class. Furthermore, class members need to feel wanted and accepted. They want to know the teacher is interested in them. Teachers need to have a passion for their lesson but equally important is their passion for the people.

> *Teachers need to have a passion for*
> *their lesson but equally important*
> *is their passion for the people.*

8. I will be faithful in tithing (giving ten percent of my gross earnings).

Tithing has kept more people from teaching Sunday School than any other issue. When I first came to serve the wonderful people of First Baptist Church Woodstock, Georgia, I sat down with my pastor, Dr. Johnny Hunt, and got his blessings on this *Sunday School Covenant*. Shortly thereafter, I was challenged on this very issue by a potential teacher. I would not permit this distinguished member to teach because he was not a tither. He appealed his case to Pastor who lovingly admonished the man to tithe and explained his support of the *Sunday School Covenant*. The man refused to follow Pastor's advice and, therefore, was not permitted to teach. Over a period of time, this issue has been a "line in the sand" for us that has been so clearly established it is seldom an issue anymore.

This issue is extremely important because I do not know how a teacher could teach a lesson on giving if he were not giving – he would be a hypocrite. Also I do not want a God robber teaching one of my Sunday School classes. (Malachi 3:8-12) Would you want a man to teach Sunday School who broke into your neighbor's house and stole from him? Of course not! Then is it permissible to steal from Almighty God and teach Sunday School but not acceptable if one steals from a mere mortal? God help us to not be "double minded" and "unstable" (James 1:8) in this matter.

I do not check their giving record; I operate on the "honor system." However, I do remind them to not lie about their giving; and I always add, "Remember Ananias and Sapphira" (Acts 5:1-11).

9. I will completely refrain from the use of alcoholic beverages.

Next to tithing, this has become the second most contested controversial issue on the *Covenant.* There was a day when you did not have to be concerned about a potential Sunday School teacher drinking alcohol. That day is now history. Many social drinkers understand the church's position against drunkenness, but they do not understand her position against social drinking. An occasional beer with the guys or a few drinks with a business client is becoming more acceptable in evangelical circles. This topic alone could be discussed in a book, so I will not take the space to address it at this time.

Here is a good rule to go by: It is better to err on the side of being squeaky-clean than to err on the side of compromise. This is true in most any area of life.

It is better to err on the side of being squeaky-clean than to err on the side of compromise.

Each church must decide for herself what standards will be upheld and what battles must be fought and what issues are important. But if we are to "abstain from all appearance of evil" (1 Thessalonians 5:22), then the consumption of alcohol qualifies as an area to flee.

10. I will attend Sunday morning and evening worship services and Wednesday evening activities unless providentially hindered.

Occasionally, a teacher becomes a "Lone Ranger" and does not see the need to participate with the rest of the body. Teachers must exemplify a team spirit. They must see themselves as one part of the body of Christ. Furthermore, they must understand the biblical admonition to join other believers in corporate worship.

11. I will be supportive of the pastor and staff.

I refuse to give someone a position of honor and influence in the church and then have them use that position to criticize the pastor or church staff. Even if the pastor or staff have made themselves vulnerable to criticism, a Sunday School class is not the place for it. A Sunday School class functions for the purpose of building people up and discipling them in the Word. It is a place to pray for one another, love one another, and support one another. It is not a place for innuendo and murmuring. If the teacher or anyone else in the class has a complaint to file with the staff, then go to the staff and voice your concern.

12. I have read and agree with the church's *Sunday School Philosophy* and will lead my class according to it.

When the choir sings during our worship services, I want them to all sing off the same sheet of music. It would be a certain calamity if they did not. Our *Sunday School Philosophy* and *Sunday School*

Covenant keep our Sunday School leadership on the "same sheet of music." Some might think we are legalistic and rigid, but I can promise you the Minister of Music is legalistic in that no other song is to be sung by a choir member other than the one selected for all. It is not a matter of legalism; it is a matter of establishing standards that come with leadership and are best for the Body of Christ.

We want to ensure our *Sunday School Philosophy* will be embraced and practiced by every member of our leadership team. It is the heart of all we do. It is the road map that keeps us from wandering on our journey to reach, teach, and minister to people. It is the heart and soul of a growing Sunday School in that it affords everyone the opportunity to understand the need to develop new leaders and birth new units. It is what helps us to involve more people in ministry and to assimilate more people. It is the compass that keeps pointing us in the right direction.

These twelve issues are non-negotiable. We do not want to compromise the integrity of our ministry. We want dedicated Christians which is the first criteria of being a good teacher and leader. As Minister of Education, it is my job to hold the standard high. Over the years, we have allowed the banner of excellence to be lowered to the point that it is now dragging the ground. As God said through the prophet Jeremiah, "Set ye up a standard in the land" (Jeremiah 51:27). We too need to re-establish some standards in our churches and in our Sunday School ministry.

We too need to re-establish some standards in our churches and in our Sunday School ministry.

After explaining the *Sunday School Philosophy* and the *Sunday School Covenant*, we go over *Truths We Hold Dear*. This document (Appendix 2) represents fifteen doctrinal statements to which we expect the teacher to adhere and comply. If a potential teacher does not embrace each of these doctrinal statements with a "strongly agree" position, then we will not let him teach. Again, this document must be developed under the leadership of your pastor. He is the one who sets the teaching agenda of the church as God's appointed shepherd for that flock of sheep.

Lastly, we have them fill out *My Personal Testimony* (Appendix 3). We want to know the salvation experience of our teachers and make sure they have been scripturally baptized. We ask the potential teaching candidate to take the three documents (*Sunday School Covenant, Truths We Hold Dear,* and *My Personal Testimony*) home and fill them out. We do not want to place any pressure on the prospect to fill these forms out to our satisfaction simply because they are in our presence. We want them to get before God and let Him direct their responses. These forms are returned at our second one-on-one meeting, and responses are discussed at that time. If the prospect eventually becomes a teacher, these three documents are placed in their personnel file. Each year we will add their annual evaluation in their personnel file as well.

As you can see, we are very intentional in placing the right people on the leadership team. These standards are used for preschool teachers to senior adult teachers. We have some guidelines for individual age divisions, but these criteria are used for all age groups. Rule of thumb in enlisting Sunday School teachers: We would rather be too thorough than not.

Examine God's Purpose

At our second individual meeting with the prospective teacher, we want to search his heart for what God is leading him to do. We want to make sure he feels called into the teaching/leading ministry of a Sunday School teacher. It is a demanding job and will be easy to quit or to put forth a half-hearted effort. If a teacher is not called, chances are they will not have longevity nor be fruitful in their service. In addition, we want to know his passion for ministry and for the particular age group he feels led to serve.

Encourage the Prospect

We share with the prospect how we came to consider him for a teacher. It may be Pastor or his current Sunday School teacher recommended him, or I may have observed his potential, etc. The point is that I want the prospect to know somebody believes in him. This is important because most people, like Moses before the burning bush, feel somewhat inferior to be a teacher and, subsequently, a public speaker. The old Chinese proverb states, "Great souls have wills; feeble ones have only wishes." Help the prospect see how he "can do all things through Christ" who strengthens him (Philippians 4:13). Your attitude toward prospects is crucial; it has the potential to make or break them. German poet, playwright, and philosopher Johann Wolfgang von Goethe (1749-1832) once said, "If you treat a man as he is, he will remain as he is; if you treat him as he ought to be and could be, he will become as he ought to be and could be."

Explain the Potential

We want the prospect to understand his opportunity to make a difference in the lives of people. We want him to know he has the privilege of binding on earth what will be "bound in heaven" (Matthew 16:19). We want him to realize the awesome privilege he has to produce fruit, more fruit, much fruit, and fruit that remains. (John 15) I believe people want to be involved in something that will make a difference. As Robert Louis Stevenson said, "To be what we are, and to become what we are capable of becoming, is the only end of life."

Big people respond to big challenges, and teaching Sunday School is no small thing. The reason some people turn out to be complacent and apathetic in their service is the lack of vision that is cast by the one enlisting. Your vision could be the start of someone's dream come true.

Employ a Plan

Set a time for a third meeting with the prospect to personally mentor the new teacher. Depending upon the individual, this could take a few meetings and phone calls. Supply him with a copy of the class roll, a current list of workers who are currently serving in some capacity in the class, and a copy of the literature; so he can become familiar and comfortable with it.

It is important to have a few times for the prospect to teach, so you can observe him and offer constructive critique. Make sure your expectations are in keeping with his lack of experience. Do not expect the prospect to be as good as your best Sunday School teacher who has been teaching for twenty years.

Equip the Person

We have developed a Teacher's Survival Kit for each age division. We use this to mentor and instruct new teachers. We want to place the new teacher in an environment for success, not failure. It is unfair to put an inexperienced teacher in front of a group of people without first doing all you can to help the new teacher experience fruitfulness and fulfillment.

As you can see, expectations are high. We see Sunday School teachers as the only people in the church who, along with the pastor, have a thirty-to forty-minute platform with our people each week. Therefore, it behooves us to place the right people in these ministry positions. We must understand that the higher the responsibility, the higher the expectations. For example, the bank custodian is not given the same expectations as the bank president; the waterboy is not burdened with the same expectations as the quarterback; a child is not expected to be as responsible as the parent. You see, the higher the responsibilities, the higher the expectations.

Your clearly stated and defined expectations will have much power and influence in the ministry of your new enlistee. We all have experienced the powerful sway of someone's expectations. As children, we experienced the influence of our parents' expectations. As students, our teachers exercised the power of expectations as revealed by our report card. Employees certainly understand the expectations of their employer. And married folks know the expectations of their spouse. Expectations are the things we presume should be done or will be done. That is why we expect it.

As Sunday School leaders, our calling soars us to new levels of responsibility and expectation. Leaders must shoulder the functions of their position. If a teacher does not carry the responsibilities of his position, then he has forfeited his right to occupy the position.

CHAPTER 5

Speaking
for God

"Then said I, Woe is me! for I am undone; because I am a man of unclean lips, and I dwell in the midst of a people of unclean lips: for mine eyes have seen the King, the LORD of hosts. Then flew one of the seraphims unto me, having a live coal in his hand, which he had taken with the tongs from off the altar: And he laid it upon my mouth, and said, Lo, this hath touched thy lips; and thine iniquity is taken away, and thy sin purged. Also I heard the voice of the Lord, saying, Whom shall I send, and who will go for us? Then said I, Here I am; send me" (Isaiah 6:5-8).

Speaking for God is a serious matter and should not be taken lightly. To stand flippantly before a class and present a lesson is a mockery to the Almighty. He has created us with the ability to use and understand words. Words are a prominent way that God communicates with us; that we communicate with Him; and that we communicate with each other.

At times, you wonder if your words have any potency. At times, getting up to teach is like trying to put out a blazing inferno with a water gun. What could I possibly say to a mother who just miscarried, to the couple who cannot get pregnant, to the parents whose child is in rebellion, to the lady whose husband just walked out on her, to the man who just lost his job? How can a theologically untrained layman teach from a 2,000-year-old document and impact a visually saturated, technologically advanced society? Who dares to "speak for God"? Yet this is our calling, and we dare not seek to disobey it: "I heard the voice of the Lord, saying, Whom shall I send, and who will go for Us?" Each week we teachers stand as God's representatives; we stand to "speak for God."

The Power of the Word of God

Let's allow the Word of God to speak for itself:

- "For the word of God is quick, and powerful, and sharper than any twoedged sword, piercing even to the dividing asunder of soul and spirit, and of the joints and marrow, and is a discerner of the thoughts and intents of the heart" (Hebrews 4:12).

- "All scripture is given by inspiration of God, and is profitable for doctrine, for reproof, for correction, for instruction in righteousness: That the man of God may be perfect, thoroughly furnished unto all good works" (2 Timothy 3:16-17).

- "For I am not ashamed of the gospel of Christ: for it is the power of God unto salvation to every one that believeth; to the Jew first, and also to the Greek" (Romans 1:16).

- "The entrance of thy words giveth light; it giveth understanding unto the simple" (Psalm 119:130).

- "Search the scriptures; for in them ye think ye have eternal life: and they are they which testify of me" (John 5:39).

- "Sanctify them through thy truth: thy word is truth" (John 17:17).

- "So then faith cometh by hearing, and hearing by the word of God" (Romans 10:17).

- "Being born again, not of corruptible seed, but of incorruptible, by the word of God, which liveth and abideth for ever" (1 Peter 1:23).

These testimonies come from the Psalmist, the Apostle Paul, the

Apostle Peter, and the Lord Jesus Christ Himself! They obviously had a strong faith in the Holy Scripture and directed their lives by it. They did not approach Scripture with a doubtful or compromising spirit. They were assured of its truth and authority. They treated it with great reverence and respect. They truly believed it to be the very oracles of the Lord God of heaven.

The Teacher's Response and Responsibility toward the Word

1. The Teacher's Attitude toward the Word

A teacher should never underestimate the power of the Word. It does have the power to transform lives. The Bible has been in the life-changing business for millennia. Therefore, a teacher should walk into the Bible study with bold confidence in the power of the Word. If a teacher does not have this confidence, then he or she should not be teaching. The Word of God is not a product we use on Sunday mornings; it is a power we allow to work in the hearts of our people. Our attitude toward the Word will have everything to do with how we teach the Word!

The Word of God is not a product we use on Sunday mornings; it is a power we allow to work in the hearts of our people.

2. The Teacher's Action with the Word

The teacher's job each week is to unleash the Word. What does a teacher do each Sunday morning? He unleashes the Word of God and turns it loose to do its eternal work in the human soul! Our action plan is to prepare and present the Word so that we do not hinder its work in the soul of man.

3. The Teacher's Appreciation for the Word

The Word must be his constant companion and the delight of his life. As Job stated, "…I have esteemed the words of his mouth more than my necessary food" (Job 23:12). As law books are to a lawyer and tools are to a mechanic, the Word of God must be to the teacher. If he is to "speak for God," then he must be constantly hearing from God.

4. The Teacher's Ammunition Is the Word of God

"And now, brethren, I commend you to God, and to the word of his grace, which is able to build you up, and to give you an inheritance among all them which are sanctified" (Acts 20:32). Paul encouraged the elders from Miletus to rely on "the word of his grace," not man's philosophies and psychology. He did not depend upon man's strategies to build people up. His sole trust was in the Word.

> "And I, brethren, when I came to you, came not with excellency of speech or of wisdom, declaring unto you the testimony of God. . . . And my speech and my preaching was not with enticing words of man's wisdom, but in demonstration of the Spirit and of power: That your faith should not stand in the wisdom of men, but in the power of God" (1 Corinthians 2:1, 4-5).

Dear teacher, when you prepare your lesson, load it full of the Word and then fire away when you present it. It is the only ammunition that can penetrate a hard heart!

5. The Teacher's Ally Is the Spirit of God

> "But as it is written, Eye hath not seen, nor ear heard, neither have 0entered into the heart of man, the things which God hath prepared for

them that love him. But God hath revealed them unto us by his Spirit: for the Spirit searcheth all things, yea, the deep things of God. For what man knoweth the things of a man, save the spirit of man which is in him? even so the things of God knoweth no man, but the Spirit of God. Now we have received, not the spirit of the world, but the Spirit which is of God; that we might know the things that are freely given to us of God. Which things also we speak, not in the words which man's wisdom teacheth, but which the Holy Ghost teacheth; comparing spiritual things with spiritual" (1 Corinthians 2:9-13).

God's Holy Spirit is the ultimate teacher.

"But the Comforter, which is the Holy Ghost, whom the Father will send in my name, he shall teach you all things, and bring all things to your remembrance, whatsoever I have said unto you" (John 14:26).

"Howbeit when he, the Spirit of truth, is come, he will guide you into all truth: for he shall not speak of himself; but whatsoever he shall hear, that shall he speak: and he will show you things to come" (John 16:13).

6. The Teacher's Audience Is the People of God

The purpose of our teaching is not to have a platform for ourselves but to serve God and others. We are there to serve God by teaching His Word and loving the people. We are there to serve the people by preparing a biblical lesson, allowing God to work within us, and then sharing with others for their benefit. Ezra, the priest of God, was faithful to present Scripture to needy people:

"And Ezra the priest brought the law before the congregation both of men and women, and all that could hear with understanding, upon the first day of the seventh month. And he read therein before the street that was before the water gate from the morning until midday, before the men and the women, and those that could understand; and the ears of all the people were attentive unto the book of the law" (Nehemiah 8:2-3).

7. The Teacher's Aim Is the Truth of God

When it comes to our lesson presentation and methodology, we should not first ask: Does it work? Does it relate? These are two valid questions. However, we must first ask: Is it true? The most important ingredient of any lesson is the presentation of truth! A teacher's most sacred trust with God is to uphold His truth. The integrity of the Word is to be maintained, and the teacher is its guardian. Once we have asked the question: Is it true?, we now can ask: Does it work? Does it relate?

The integrity of the Word is to be maintained, and the teacher is its guardian.

"When a prophet speaketh in the name of the LORD, if the thing follow not, nor come to pass, that is the thing which the LORD hath not spoken, but the prophet hath spoken it presumptuously: thou shalt not be afraid of him" (Deuteronomy 18:22).

The Power of the Teacher's Words

1. Words can minister healing.

"A man hath joy by the answer of his mouth: and a word spoken in due season, how good is it!" (Proverbs 15:23)

Teachers need to understand the power of their words. People attend your class because they like you. They have entrusted you with the right to influence them. I remember addressing a lady's question about the role of the man and woman in the home. She had been out of church and had persuasions that would have made the feminist movement proud. Yet over time, she "bought in" to scriptural instruction on the subject because she trusted me and my desire to hold the Word as the highest authority.

The reason healing is needed is because our classes are full of wounded people. Sin leaves wounds, and these spiritual wounds need spiritual medicine.

2. Words can minister harm.

"How long will ye vex my soul, and break me in pieces with words?" (Job 19:2)

Words also can cause much damage. To misrepresent the Word of God can create ruin in the lives of people. I have seen the results of some teachers who did not regard the Word as God would have intended. It leaves many spiritually crippled for life.

The Word often hurts for a season, so it can ultimately produce health in the life of a spiritually wounded person. Like the shot you receive from the doctor, its temporary hurt is necessary for the permanent healing it brings.

3. The teacher's words have the power to change lives.

"A word fitly spoken is like apples of gold in pictures of silver" (Proverbs 25:11).

Blaise Pascal, the French mathematician, physicist, and philosopher, said, "Cold words freeze people, and hot words scorch them, and bitter words make them bitter, and wrathful words make them wrathful. Kind words also produce their own image on men's souls; and a beautiful image it is. They soothe and quiet and comfort the hearer."

God-called teachers live for those moments when they stand confidently and proclaim, "I have a word from the Lord."

The Teacher as a Wordsmith

Since words are the tools of our trade, we must know how to use them. We must craft them in a way that is useful to those who will hear them and use them. Therefore, teachers are "wordsmiths"— craftsmen who need to become masters of their trade.

Teachers are "wordsmiths."

There are many myths about communicating. Public speaking has been tagged as the greatest fear that people encounter which has given occasion to the rise of many communication myths. These myths have spooked off many potential Bible teachers in our Sunday School classes. Let's examine some of these myths.

Myth 1: Communication is only for the well educated.

"Now when they saw the boldness of Peter and John, and perceived that they were unlearned and ignorant men, they marveled; and they took knowledge of them, that they had been with Jesus" (Acts 4:13).

Obviously, the more educated a person is, the greater the potential to be a good teacher. The base for all teaching is content knowledge. Ignorance certainly is not bliss. The first hurdle to clear in teaching is to know something which is the foundation of all teaching. The ability to communicate knowledge then becomes the second hurdle to jump. Many knowledgeable people are poor teachers because they lack the ability to present their knowledge in a way that connects with the learner.

The base for all teaching is content knowledge.

To assume only the well educated can teach is shortsighted. The issue at stake is not how well educated you are but are you still learning. Simply put, learners are teachers. If content knowledge is the base of all teaching, then teachers need to be the best and most progressive learners in the class. It is not good enough to survive on yesterday's knowledge. Do not feed your class stale bread left over from days gone by; bake them fresh, hot bread. When you feed fresh bread, people will show up at meal time.

Myth 2: Communication is the mere exchanging of information.

"Thy word have I hid in mine heart, that I might not sin against thee" (Psalm 119:11).

"Thy word is a lamp unto my feet, and a light unto my path" (Psalm 119:105).

Communicating the Word of God innately releases truth, power, life, and transformation. If not, then we are merely cheap politicians, peddling our ideologies on others. The Bible is filled with information, but information alone will not change a life. Truth, on the other hand, will.

> *Communicating the Word of God*
> *innately releases truth, power,*
> *life, and transformation.*

Myth 3: Communication is all in the words.

"But be ye doers of the word, and not hearers only, deceiving your own selves" (James 1:22).

Communication travels on the modeling you provide. Truth is transferred by example. Your life speaks much louder than your lips. The Apostle Paul told the church at Corinth: "Be ye followers of me" (1 Corinthians 4:16; 11:1).

If words equaled communication, then our children should understand everything! Words are great vehicles in transferring truth but not the only way to convey thought. When Jesus wanted to teach servanthood, He took a towel and a basin of water and washed the disciples' feet. (John 13:1-16) When He wanted to teach humility, He received little children. (Mark 10:14-16) When He wanted to teach that He could forgive sin, He healed a man with palsy. (Mark 2:1-12) Words, coupled with example and illustration, make a powerful communication tool.

Myth 4: Communication is the result of many words.

"Then the LORD answered Job out of the whirlwind, and said, Who is this that darkeneth counsel by words without knowledge?" (Job 38:1-2)

Words without knowledge are worse than no words at all. The old country proverb provides good advice: "It is better to keep your mouth shut and have people think you are a fool than to open it and remove all doubt!" Using many words can be a deterrent to communication. It has been said that lawyers are the only people in the world who can write something 10,000 words long and call it a brief. The issue is not to count your words but to make your words count! Communication is not dependent upon the length of your words but the strength of your words!

Communication is not dependent upon the length of your words but the strength of your words!

People grow weary with wordiness and senseless talk. The book of Job exemplifies much talk on the part of Job's three friends. There is a constant volley of words being batted back and forth with little accomplishment. Finally, exasperated with all of the words, Job asks, "Shall vain words have an end?..." (Job 16:3) He further states he is "weary" with it all. (Job 16:7) He probably represents the sentiments of many Sunday School attendees who must endure a battery of impotent arsenals that are misaimed each week.

Sometimes when I fly back into Atlanta, the pilot will have to circle the airport a few times before waiting his turn to land. I am not impressed with his ability to circle the airport. Once I arrive at my destination, I want to land. So it is with your learners. They are not impressed with the amount of verbiage you can use. They want you to make your point and then land that baby. As someone has suggested, "Let your yea be yea, your nay be nay, and your 'in conclusion' be your conclusion."

Myth 5: Communication is derived from using fine-tuned techniques.

"For we have not followed cunningly devised fables, when we made known unto you the power and coming of our Lord Jesus Christ..." (2 Peter 1:16).

As important as methodology is, it will never supercede authenticity! I have heard speakers who butchered the "king's English" but were so real and spoke from the heart that they greatly transferred their passion into my soul. On the other hand, I have heard those who were "slicked up and polished down" but could not move me one step closer to God or His will. I think authenticity is the missing ingredient in our Bible teaching today. Our lessons ride on the rails of trust; and when the rails are damaged, the train will be destroyed. We have those who attempt to teach the Word without first living it, who "talk it" but don't "walk it," who proclaim it but don't practice it. In essence, we make ourselves hypocrites and become like the Pharisees.

Our lessons ride on the rails of trust.

Myth 6: God wants you to be a powerful communicator.

"And I was with you in weakness, and in fear, and in much trembling" (1 Corinthians 2:3).

God does not need a powerful communicator; He needs a powerful message! He imparts no power to enhance our audience with clout or attraction. He is not impressed with our charisma or charm. He desires to give authority only to those obedient souls who are committed to His agenda and purposes. Therefore, His ultimate goal for every teacher is to be an obedient follower.

• Moses felt inferior as a communicator.

"And Moses said unto the LORD, O my Lord, I am not eloquent, neither heretofore, nor since thou hast spoken unto thy servant: but I am slow of speech, and of a slow tongue" (Exodus 4:10).

• Jeremiah acknowledged his inability to speak.

"Then said I, Ah, Lord GOD! behold, I cannot speak: for I am a child" (Jeremiah 1:6).

In both of these cases, God was not looking for an eloquent speaker. Instead He was looking for a submissive, obedient child! We live in a day when charisma is more favored than wisdom. I see many preachers and teachers who have phenomenal charisma and personality. It is a gift from God and ought to be used for His glory. However, charisma falls short of achieving the esteemed rank—unlike wisdom.

> "Get wisdom, get understanding: forget it not; neither decline from the words of my mouth. Forsake her not, and she shall preserve thee: love her, and she shall keep thee. Wisdom is the principal thing; therefore get wisdom: and with all thy getting get understanding" (Proverbs 4:5-7).

The wisest man who ever lived next to the Lord Jesus Christ was Solomon, and he did not admonish us to get charisma. Instead he said, "Get wisdom." God does not need you to be powerful, charismatic, or gifted. He needs you to be wise because "a wise man will hear, and will increase learning; and a man of understanding shall attain unto wise counsels" (Proverbs 1:5). Your wise words will be esteemed by others.

> "When the ear heard me, then it blessed me...Unto me men gave ear, and waited, and kept silence at my counsel. After my words they spake not again; and my speech dropped upon them" (Job 29:11, 21-22).

We not only need to know the myths of communication, but we need to know how to master communication. I want to suggest five simple ways that a teacher can begin to communicate truth and become an effective "wordsmith."

Step 1: By understanding the Scriptures.

> "And Philip ran thither to him, and heard him read the prophet Isaiah, and said, *Understandest thou what thou readest?* And he said, How can I, *except some man should guide me?* And he desired Philip that he would come up and sit with him. ...Then Philip opened his mouth, and began at the same scripture, and preached unto him Jesus" (Acts 8:30-31, 35, *emphasis mine*).

We dealt with this earlier, but it bears repetition. Content of the subject matter is essential in mastering your ability to communicate to others. Philip's knowledge of Isaiah 53 had everything to do with his ability to explain it to the Ethiopian eunuch and see him come to faith in Christ. The basis of his communication was knowing the content of the passage. Mark it down and make it clear – a Bible teacher must be a student of the Word of God. There are no substitutes for your knowledge of Scripture.

A Bible teacher must be a student of the Word of God.

Step 2: By living what you teach.

"Whosoever therefore shall break one of these least commandments, and shall teach men so, he shall be called the least in the kingdom of heaven: but whosoever shall do and teach them, the same shall be called great in the kingdom of heaven" (Matthew 5:19).

Years ago, I had the blessing of hearing L. C. Roberts preach. Rev. Roberts was an old man who had pastored for many years and was forced into retirement by a heart attack. He would preach at our church when our pastor was on vacation. The thing that always impressed me about his preaching was the evidence of his personal conviction about the message he was proclaiming. He had little trouble convincing me of biblical truth because he was so convinced of it himself. The convictions he preached had first gripped his own heart and now found easy passage to my heart. I also was touched, moved, and stirred by this humble, old man who stood with a Bible in his hand and a conviction in his heart. O, to God that we had more Bible teachers like L. C. Roberts!

Step 3: By being passionate.

"Whatsoever thy hand findeth to do, do it with thy might..." (Ecclesiastes 9:10).

Teaching God's Word should never be humdrum. Our class graces us with the privilege of teaching them for a period of time. After this time has expired, we must have earned the right to teach them or we will lose them. Job said, "Doth not the ear try words?..." (12:11) The question then becomes: Do we deserve the ears of our class? Our class will become indifferent and apathetic to the Word only if we do. Our attitude and approach to the Word will be received by our class. Our approach should be one of enthusiasm and invigoration because the Word of God is:

- Eternal

"Forever, O LORD, thy word is settled in heaven" (Psalm 119:89).

- Exalted

"I will worship toward thy holy temple, and praise thy name for thy loving-kindness and for thy truth: for thou hast magnified thy word above all thy name" (Psalm 138:2).

Peter teaches that as babies desire milk, so should new Christians "desire the sincere milk of the word" (1 Peter 2:2). If a baby Christian ought to have a thirst for the Word, then how much more should we who teach it!

Step 4: By applying Scripture to everyday life.

"For the commandment is a lamp; and the law is light; and reproofs of instruction are the way of life" (Proverbs 6:23).

Recently, I had some friends who became empty-nesters and were downsizing their house. Their new and smaller home could not house all of their furniture from their former residence, so they stored some furniture in a rented storage unit. We often teach Bible lessons with a storage facility mentality. We store biblical facts and information instead of using this knowledge. Unlike an overabundance of furniture, Scripture is not to be laid up in storage; it is to be applied and used every day. Our class members want to know if this lesson will help them on Monday morning when they hit the streets.

Step 5: By using stories.

"The same day went Jesus out of the house, and sat by the sea side. And great multitudes were gathered together unto him, so that he went into a ship, and sat; and the whole multitude stood on the shore. And he spake many things unto them in parables..." (Matthew 13:1-3).

Jesus used the medium of parables to translate godly truth. He extracted heavenly principles from earthly stories. Abraham Lincoln may have learned this teaching aid from his Scripture reading. He once said, "They say I tell a great many stories. I reckon I do; but I have learned from long experience that plain people, take them as they run, are more easily influenced through the medium of a broad and humorous illustration than in any other way."

Communication Defined

Communication is the transfer of thought from one individual to another. The thought is conceived in the mind, heart, and soul of the teacher and translated to the mind, heart, and soul of the learner by the vehicle of words and life. In the setting of a Sunday School class, communication is conveyed in a linear sequence that originates with the teacher, is empowered by his example, travels through the lesson, and into the learner. Communication is a contact sport! The teacher makes contact with the learner through the channel of his lesson and his life. The teacher's example of making contact is Christ Himself as He becomes the embodiment of God.

Communication is a contact sport!

The Incarnation Principle

Truth, principles, and precepts cannot be communicated and translated unless they are "fleshed out." Truth is translated to others by living more than speaking. As Dr. James Dobson has said, "Principles are caught, not taught." We cannot expect people to believe what we talk if it is not consistent with our walk. Howard Hendricks has correctly stated, "Most of us teach above our living."

The greatest example of this concept is God Himself. When God wanted to express truth to mankind, He rolled it all up in the life of His Son. Jesus was always God: "In the beginning was the Word, and the Word was with God, and the Word was God. The same was in the beginning with God. All things were made by him; and without him was not any thing made that was made" (John 1:1-3). God knew in order to convey Himself, His principles, His truth, He had to flesh them out. Mankind would never grasp His teachings until they were "fleshed out." He could not mold us into His principles until He modeled them for us. Therefore, "And the Word was made flesh, and dwelt among us...the only begotten Son, which is in the bosom of the Father, he hath declared him" (John 1:14, 18). All that God had for the world was wrapped up in a package of eight or nine pounds of flesh: The Babe of Bethlehem!

God used other vehicles to express Himself to the people whom He loved
so much. However, there was something lacking—imperfection could

not adequately communicate perfection. Man was teaching above his living. So God sent His perfect Son so that truth could be perfectly transmitted.

"God, who at sundry times and in divers manners spake in time past unto the fathers by the prophets, Hath in these last days spoken unto us by his Son, whom he hath appointed heir of all things, by whom also he made the worlds; Who being the brightness of his glory, and the express image of his person, and upholding all things by the word of his power, when he had by himself purged our sins, sat down on the right hand of the Majesty on high" (Hebrews 1:1-3).

We will never teach like Jesus; but the more we become like Him, the more effective our teaching will become. We will be great *proclaimers* of God's principles only when we become great *practitioners* of God's principles. You see, truth must be wrapped in flesh! In Sunday School, truth is all packaged up in the person of the teacher.

> *We will be great proclaimers of God's*
> *principles only when we become great*
> *practitioners of God's principles.*

Jesus taught this principle, and He placed our living before our teaching:

> "Whosoever therefore shall break one of these least commandments, and shall teach men so, he shall be called the least in the kingdom of heaven: but whosoever shall do and teach them, the same shall be called great in the kingdom of heaven" (Matthew 5:19).

Truths to Ponder

1. The "Word" (Greek *logos*) was God's ultimate vehicle of communication.

2. The "Word" was to be communicated through embodying flesh.

3. The "Word" was to dwell with people, inferring relationships to be established.

4. God speaks.

5. God has spoken in different times and in different ways.

6. God's ultimate communication to man came through Jesus, "the express image of His person."

7. The more we "conform to His image," the more effective we become in "speaking for God."

CHAPTER 6

Lesson Planning

Tom Landry, former coach of the Dallas Cowboys, said, "The will to practice is greater than the will to win." When I first heard this statement, I was an assistant high school football coach myself, and I really scratched my head. I thought the greatest desire a person should have is the will to win. Yet the more I thought and meditated on what Coach Landry said, the more I realized he was right. If you practice well and prepare well, then the game will take care of itself.

This is true when teaching a Sunday School lesson. The issue is not how charismatic and dynamic you are, but are you ready for kickoff? Many teams with superior talent have lost because they were not ready for kickoff. Just showing up does not win football games nor does it make you capable of teaching a good lesson. When I coached, Steve Brewer, our head coach, would often be asked after Thursday night's final practice: "Coach, are we ready for tomorrow night's game?" Steve would always reply, "The hay is in the barn. If we are not ready now, we're not going to be." Coach Brewer understood that if our players were not prepared after our last time of preparation, we were in for trouble the next evening. The hay was in the barn. Teacher, when you show up on Sunday morning, the hay is already in the barn. You have already prepared yourself for that special time on Sunday morning.

Obviously, Coach Landry and Coach Brewer both realized that the need to prepare paved the way to victory. So it is with teaching; the greatest teachers are the best prepared teachers. Nothing, absolutely nothing, can replace your personal preparation time. Everyone is interested in winning. However, not every one is committed to do what it takes to win. Every Sunday School teacher wants to teach good lessons, but every Sunday School teacher is not committed to do what it takes to have good lessons. They have not put any hay in the barn during the week, so the loft is empty on Sunday morning. If you are committed to preparation, you will be a great Sunday School teacher.

The greatest teachers
are the best prepared teachers.

Lesson preparation is so important because the impact of your teaching is in direct proportion to your preparation and the change in the lives of your class members is in direct proportion to your teaching. It also becomes important from the standpoint that it is a major part of what you do each week as a teacher. Preparation is important for all ages. Oftentimes we think there are some ages that we tolerate and there are other ages that we teach. This is not true. Every age should be taught—from the bed babies all the way up through senior adults. Now I know we cannot teach everyone the same, but everyone should come to church and learn. The Word of God is the hub around which everything we do centers and revolves—whether it is in the worship service or in Sunday School. There are many other things that take place, but the Word of God is the center focus of everything we do when we meet. That being the case, there must be intensive preparation for our time of Bible study.

Myth: The key to great teaching is great ability.

I do not want to undermine ability. Obviously, we all want great ability. Talent and ability are great tools in God's hand, but ability alone will not make you a good Sunday School teacher.

Truth: The key to great teaching is great preparation.

Again, ability is beneficial; but it is not everything. Preparedness is what makes the decided difference. Why did Peter, James, and John become great teachers? Because they were multi-talented? I am not so sure they were. They spent three and a half years being prepared by the Master. I believe this was the difference maker in their ministries.

Proper, prior, purposeful preparation prevents pitifully poor, pathetic presentations! To be a good Sunday School teacher, you do not have to hit home runs every Sunday; but you must consistently hit singles. Most preachers do not hit a home run with every sermon. If you can consistently hit singles by consistently teaching and giving people the Word of God, you can be a successful teacher. It really is true that chance favors the prepared mind. God gave you a mind and expects you to use it for something besides a hat rack.

- "Jesus said unto him, Thou shalt love the Lord thy God with all thy heart, and with all thy soul, and with all thy mind" (Matthew 22:37).

- "These were more noble than those in Thessalonica, in that they received the word with all readiness of mind, and searched the scriptures daily, whether those things were so" (Acts 17:11).

- "And be not conformed to this world: but be ye transformed by the renewing of your mind, that ye may prove what is that good, and acceptable, and perfect, will of God" (Romans 12:2).

- "For God hath not given us the spirit of fear; but of power, and of love, and of a sound mind" (2 Timothy 1:7).

- "...I will put my laws into their mind..." (Hebrews 8:10).

- "Wherefore gird up the loins of your mind..." (1 Peter 1:13).

I am afraid that Satan is winning so many victories in our lives because he has won the battle for our minds. For this reason, you ought to guard your mind and be careful what you put into it. Your mind is important.

Therefore, constantly seek to improve. Always accept the challenge to be stretched. Allow yourself to be taken out of your comfort zone occasionally. The mind is a wonderful thing, so don't waste it. The old saying applies here: "Minds are like parachutes; they only work when open!" Your mind is the tool God has given you to use to prepare, so use it.

The three keys to a successful lesson:

Key 1: Prepare!

Key 2: Prepare!!

Key 3: Prepare!!!

Preparation IS the key to a successful lesson!

The brain has two parts: the left side and the right side. The left side is the logical, analytical side of the brain. It judges, selects, applies logic, and puts things in proper sequences and categories. The right side is the creative side. It explores, entertains, fantasizes, provokes, and generates.

Both sides are needed for a good lesson.

- The left side gives substance, content, and continuity to the lesson.

- The right side gives excitement and energy to the lesson.

Each side complements the other. As the wings of an airplane are both needed and complement the other, a good lesson will incorporate both sides of the brain and will involve and stimulate the various people who learn differently.

The following lessons can be categorized as "left-brain lessons" or "right-brain lessons" or, in some cases, "no brain." You make the call.

- The Cotton Candy Lesson: Very sweet and full of air but when bitten into – nothing there.

- The Stuffed Olive Lesson: Pleasantly fashioned, pleasing tart stuffed with intellect – but no heart.

- The Jello Fruit Salad Lesson: Shaking, prancing, quivering preaching; lots of action – but low-calorie teaching.

- The Poached Egg Lesson: Soft, sage, sentimental food; soothes every mind, calms every mood.

- The Leftover Turkey Lesson: Meat they suspect you've served them before but disguised just enough for one Sunday more.

- The Meat and Potatoes Lesson: Exciting flare and always good; the gospel preached with the Word understood. I want to sit under a teacher who can feed me the "meat and potatoes" of the Word.

As we think about this, let's look at several factors that shape teachers.

1. *Most teachers use only the left side of their brain in preparing and presenting lessons* – the reason being it is the side of the brain that largely enables us to analyze content and assimilate that content into a presentable form. The gift of teaching seems to lend itself more to the left side than it does to the right.

2. *Most teachers give the majority of their attention to the content of the lesson with little thought on the presentation.* This is natural; for without proper content, the method of teaching is meaningless. Biblical content is the most vital ingredient of any lesson. It is the basis upon which all else revolves. It is the foundation of truth, righteousness, and godly living. So it is most healthy to begin preparing by analyzing the biblical text. But after doing a thorough exegesis of the text, give consideration to the presentation and methodology of conveying the passage to your learners. If you expound great truths but it connects with no one, then the question must be asked: "Have you really taught?" Can we honestly say teaching has taken place if learning has not occurred? The opposite is certainly true: having wonderful style and interesting methods but little substance is to abort the teaching/learning process.

3. *Teachers usually teach the way they learn.* Whatever style is best suited to your learning is probably the style you use when teaching. This is most natural. However, everyone in your class does not learn the same way you do. Therefore, the more styles you use, the more people you connect with God's truth.

You teach the way you learn. If you learn well under a lecturer, then in all likelihood, you will lecture when you teach. If you learn through visuals, then you will use visuals in your teaching. Teachers fall into the trap of using the same teaching method over and over because they become comfortable and conformable to that. You need to be stretched and challenged to try something different. This means you will risk failure, and it is permissible to fail. We have feared failure so much in our churches that we have become stale, stagnant, and status-quo driven.

4. *The teacher's employment of different methodologies is minimized with a large class.* The larger the class, the more difficult it becomes to incorporate different teaching/learning styles. The larger the class becomes, the more your style is dictated to you. It is logistically hard to break a large class into groups, have them work on assignments, and report back. The bigger the class gets, the more confining it is in teaching style. However, every teacher needs to use as many styles as possible so that they reach as many people as possible when they teach.

5. *The worst method a teacher can use is the same one.* I have often heard people say the worst method of teaching is lecture. I disagree. If lecture is wrong, then preaching is wrong. What is preaching? What is a sermon? It is a lecture. You do not break into buzz groups and brainstorming sessions during the sermon time. It is a lecture. So if lecture is wrong, preaching is wrong. Since we know preaching is not wrong, so lecture is not wrong. Thousands of churchgoers make their way to worship every Sunday all over the globe to hear a lecture, and we want to call that wrong? If you have a boring lecturer, then we may have an argument against preaching sermons. Instead I want to suggest the worst teaching method is the same one used over and over again. This means you are hitting only a particular segment of your group that learns best with that method. So mix it up a little, and do not become so predictable.

We have looked at the makeup of a teacher, but let's look at the makeup of the learners who may be in your class. There are three keys for effective learning.

1. *Repetition*

Give it to them over and over and over again. When I coached, there were certain drills I put my players through almost daily. I wanted them to be able to execute those techniques in their sleep. As a coach, I was creating a second nature in them. When it comes game time and you have to react in a split second, you do not have time to think about that technique; you must respond with an involuntary reaction. You do it because it is inbred in you.

Well, the more we have repetition, the more we learn. Repetition is not wrong. In fact, every elementary teacher knows the value of repetition with her students. How many times does a mother instruct her children to use good manners, be respectful, be polite, etc.? The repetition of basic truths is necessary to properly train a child, but this is also true of teenagers and adults.

2. *Object Lessons*

Preschool, elementary, and even youth teachers are usually pretty good at using object lessons; but adult teachers tremble at the thought of it. A child learns more in early childhood than he ever does as an adult. How is a child taught in early childhood? By object lessons.

I remember a lesson I taught a thirty- to thirty-five-year-old class. We were looking at John 17:14-18. Our central Bible truth was we were to be in the world but not of the world. That morning I illustrated our central Bible truth with an object lesson. I brought out a glass half full of water and a quart of 10W30 motor oil. I then proceeded to pour the motor oil into the glass. The oil just stood on top of the water without intermingling with it. I commented that even as oil and water do not mix, neither do Christians and the world. This visual illustrated perfectly we are to be in the world but not of the world. Ten years later, Tony Kellam, a member of that class, attended one of my conferences. During one of the breaks, he mentioned that illustration and the biblical truth taught by it. On that particular Sunday morning, I know I taught a great lesson. I am sure I was very eloquent in speech. I am sure I had a tremendous outline with points and subpoints, but all Tony remembered was the object lesson! A decade later, he recalled it with uncanny clarity.

I remember my cousin, Carole Gorman, taught the children's sermon every week. She did a tremendous job. I remember her teaching the kids one Sunday to guard your tongue, to be careful what you say. To illustrate, she took a tube of toothpaste and squirted some of the paste on a plate. She then handed it to one of the children and asked the child to put it back into the tube. The child giggled and then informed Carole that you could not put the paste back in after it was out. Carole replied, "You can't. Neither can you retract your words once they are out. Once they go out of your mouth, you can never bring them back." I don't remember another thing Carole said that day; but decades later, I remember her object lesson.

3. *Variety*

Sometime variety is just as simple as setting your room up differently. A couple had been visiting our church and our class for a few weeks. As they entered the Sunday School room one morning, he said, "Allan, this is the fifth straight Sunday we have attended this class; and it is the fifth straight Sunday that it has been set up differently." Do you know what he had just told me? Something is going to happen in here this morning! Someone is prepared and has a game plan for our time together. He knew there would be no "Leftover Turkey" for the lesson that day. The hay was in the barn.

The more variety used by the teacher, the more learning takes place. Variety adds several things:

A. Connection

Learners connect when variety is used because it forces them to participate in the learning process. As more methods are used, connection to the central Bible truth becomes more easily grasped.

B. Anticipation

Learners should come to Bible study with a spirit of anticipation. This creates a sense of interest in the learner.

C. Involvement

The more variety you use, the more people involve themselves in the lesson. Principle: A truth told is fast past, but a truth discov-

Principle: A truth told is fast past, but a truth discovered will last and last!

ered will last and last!

D. Excitement

My mother used to say, "Variety is the spice of life." It is also the spice of a Sunday School class. Use it some, and you will not have to worry about your class becoming bored. I had a godly man tell me he was becoming bored with his church. He said, "If I am sick and at home on Sunday morning, I can look at my clock and tell you exactly what they are doing because it is the same thing they always do." The study of God's Word ought not to be boring. Shame on the teacher that takes that which is "quick, and powerful, and sharper than any twoedged sword" (Hebrews 4:12) and makes it "dead, and weak, and duller than a butter knife."

Dare to be Creative

Get out of your comfort zone, and dare to teach in new ways. The 19th century philosopher Soren Kiekegaard said, "To dare is to lose one's footing only temporarily; to not dare is to lose one's self." I believe most people have gifts and abilities that lie dormant within them because they never gain the sense of security to risk failure in order to explore new possibilities. We naturally gravitate to safe turf.

I believe most people have gifts and abilities that lie dormant within them because they never gain the sense of security to risk failure in order to explore new possibilities.

Commitment to the norm may not be commitment at all. Are you committed to teaching? This I know: I am committed to teaching in my air-conditioned, carpeted Sunday School room with the wonderful friends I have in my class. But am I committed to teaching in the fields of Africa or the slums of the inner city or in a halfway house? Religious writer Thomas Merton said, "Commitment without personal jeopardy is meaningless activity." Do we teach out of commitment or convenience?

Jesus taught on a mountainside, from a boat pushed out from shore, in the synagogues, on the streets, in houses, in wheat fields, vineyards, with children in His lap, in an upper room, and even on the cross. Jesus was committed to teaching!

Anyone who has taught has blown it from time to time. Everyone has lessons that seem to go flat—even Babe Ruth struck out. Today professional baseball players are paid millions of dollars a year to get a hit only three out of ten times they bat. So do not fear fear. Step up to the plate, and take a few swings. If you strike out today, you will still get another chance next Sunday. The best way to have a great idea is to always have ideas.

• Failure is an event, not a person.

You say, "Allan, I'm going to take your challenge; and next week I'm going to teach my class differently. I'm going to try some different teaching styles and methods." After the lesson, you say, "Man, that was a flop." So that does not make you a failure. You just tried something different, and it did not work.

Do you ladies ever try a new recipe and your husband does not like it? That does not make you a failure. It means he did not have good taste. Right? So next week if you try something different and they do not like it, they just have bad taste. It will take your learners a little while to adjust. Remember, you have conditioned them to do the same thing and expect the same things. It may take a few Sundays for them to catch on – so persevere.

Attitudes Needed in Preparation

1. You must believe that what you are preparing to teach:

A. Has the power to change lives. (Isaiah 55:11; Hebrews 4:12) And if it does not, then why are you teaching it? You ought to believe your lesson has the power to change lives. That excites me because I realize the transforming power of the Word of God. That is why I jump at the opportunity to teach. To impact a person and see change in him is what floats my boat. The Word does not return void, according to Isaiah 55:11.

B. Is the eternal Word of God. (Psalm 119:89, 152) Again, if it is not, why are you teaching it?

C. Has the ability to keep people from sin. "Thy word have I hid in my heart, that I might not sin against thee" (Psalm 119:11).

D. Gives hope for everyday living. (Psalm 119:43, 49, 74, 81, 116, 147) If we did not teach for any other reason but to give hope, that would be enough. Without hope, life becomes unbearable.

2. You must ask yourself two important questions:

Does the class exist for me? Or do I exist for the class? Remember, we are dealing with attitudes needed in preparation. If your class will learn more by you teaching with different styles, then that you must do. If you are unwilling, then you have told me a lot about your attitude about your class.

Does the class exist for me? The attitude exposed: It's my place to perform for Christ.

Do I exist for the class? The attitude exposed: It's their place to conform to Christ.

It is not about how you perform but about how they conform.

It is not about how you perform but about how they conform. Teach with that in mind, and you will be a life-changing teacher.

Preparation Is a Discipline

Preparation is not so much a skill as it is an attitude of discipline. Preparation is grind time. You put your nose to the grindstone and burn the midnight oil. You spend many hours studying and meditating over Scripture. Discipline is the great separator of teachers.

Teaching what you have prepared is prime time. You should feel ready to go by Sunday morning because you have studied diligently. You have put much labor in the fields of preparation and have come to the barn with a full loft of hay. There is no glory in grind time—just blood, sweat, and tears. No one knows the joy of personal time alone with God and His Word like a dedicated Sunday School teacher. He has been refreshed and nourished in the Word and takes pleasure in the spiritual prosperity of his labor.

As a high school coach, I always looked forward to Friday night (well, most of the time). After a hard week of preparation, I was ready to go. I used to take great pride in studying film, putting a game plan together, and then instilling it into my players at practice. Come Friday night, I felt I was at my best. It was prime time. It was time to unleash all that had gone into grind time.

There are five disciplines that must be exercised to be properly prepared for a lesson.

1.   Study time (2 Timothy 2:15)

The discipline to break free of the world and its cares in order to study is the first major hurdle one must clear to be a good teacher. My players had to be at practice running and sweating and hitting, while the other students were enjoying more leisure moments. So it is with the discipline of studying. Preparation time is perspiration time! My rule of thumb is a minimum of two hours of study for every ten minutes I must teach. If I have a forty-minute lesson, I have got to have at least eight hours of preparation. Maybe you can move at a faster pace, but I want to move slow. I want a slow, steady shower of rain that can soak in rather than a quick, hard downpour that mostly runs off. I want to cook my lesson in the crock pot, not the microwave.

I want to cook my lesson in the crock pot,

not the microwave.

2. Prayer (Psalm 119:33-40)

We need God to prepare our hearts and condition us to receive from Him what He is trying to teach us. Once the Holy Spirit teaches us, we are ready to teach out of the overflow.

3. Meditation (Psalm 119:15, 97, 99, 148)

Meditation is something we ignore today in our hurry-up, hustle-and-bustle world; but, oh, how we need to meditate on the Word of God. My definition of the word *meditate* is "soak." Just soak in the Word of God. I believe David meditated a lot on the Word out in the shepherd fields. This practice transformed him and gave him such a renewed mind that he could face the giant Goliath when no one else could. Meditating is like sitting in a great, big tub of water and just soaking in it.

4. Excellence (Ecclesiastes 9:10)

Have the discipline not only to prepare but to prepare for excellence. Many times my players would just go through the motions of practicing. Jim Parker, the former great lineman with the then Baltimore Colts, said every day when he walked out of the gates of the practice field, he would ask himself if he was a better player than he was the day before. If the answer was no, he continued practicing until he was.

What I am attempting to expound is this: Don't settle for an ill-prepared lesson. When you walk into the classroom on Sunday morning, you ought to feel you have the best lesson you could put together. Now I understand that some lessons come together much easier than others. And conversely, some lessons come much harder than others. But if I am a member of your class, I want to know you have put forth your best effort to feed me that day. I don't want a "Saturday night special." Once I was in a class running about eighteen, and the gentleman teaching it grew it down to about six. Why? He never studied. It was obvious he had not studied and prepared to teach "the unsearchable riches of Christ" (Ephesians 3:8).

When you walk into the classroom on
Sunday morning, you ought to feel you have
the best lesson you could put together.

5. Longevity (Isaiah 28:9-10, 13)

Longevity is a discipline we must exercise if we are going to be good teachers. When you first start teaching, you are not going to be as good a teacher as you will be in five years. So do not get discouraged. Do not expect to be a great teacher after a few months. You have to go through that discipline of learning how to prepare and present a lesson. A ball player does not become great after a few practices and games. It is a pursuit of many years, many trials, many failures, and many attempts. Many new teachers become disheartened and quit after a year or two when they are just on the verge of breaking through. It takes time to get your arms around teaching and to refine it. So be prepared to stick around awhile and perfect your trade.

Think about the growth process. Isaiah said it was "line upon line" and "precept upon precept" (Isaiah 28:13). We could paraphrase this and apply it to say "lesson upon lesson." You learn the Bible one lesson at a time. Simple mathematics reveals you teach approximately fifty lessons a year. After two years, you have taught 100 lessons; after five years, you would have studied and taught 250 lessons. As I write this, my mother has just completed fifty-three years of teaching Sunday School. She has taught about 2,650 lessons. This is how you become a great teacher. Longevity is vital in your pursuit to know the Word and to communicate the Word!

Three Parts to a Lesson

1. Motivation

Understand that people are not focused on the Bible lesson when they walk into your class on Sunday morning. Their minds have been occupied on getting up on time, preparing breakfast, what to wear, helping with the kids, etc. Their mind is a hundred miles away from the truth they will encounter from God's Word that day. My favorite cartoon shows a man sitting in the car and blowing the horn. It is obvious he is mad. The door of the car opens; and his wife stands there with a baby in her arms, a toddler standing at her side, and a diaper bag draped over her shoulder. She eyes her husband with a look of disgust and says, "Next Sunday I'll sit out here and blow the horn, while you get the kids ready." I am afraid this is the experience of most who come to your Sunday School class. Their mind is not on the central Bible truth of your lesson. So it is up to you to kick their brain into gear.

Let me refer to my coaching years once again. Each day I started practice with a drill that required physical exertion. They had to run; they had to hit each other. I wanted them to break a good sweat and get the blood pumping. This would get them "into" practice; it would engage them and help them forget about the fight they just had with their girlfriend. Then I would teach them new plays, formations, etc. for a game plan that week. If they had just walked down to practice after they got out of class (and probably slept through half of it), they would not have been mentally and emotionally conditioned to learn. You see, you have to do something when they come into that classroom to engage the class mentally and emotionally into the lesson.

2. Examination

What are you going to do to study God's Word? How will you examine Bible truth? The *Motivation* part of the lesson plan sets the stage for this *Examination* phase of the lesson. The teacher has studied the Scripture text and now prepares for the learners to participate in ways that help them grasp biblical truths themselves. More time should be devoted to this part of the lesson than the other two parts. At this juncture, the learner should get into the meat of the Word. The learner should be confronted with: "What does this mean?" He should then be guided into discovering the proper interpretation of the text.

Here are fourteen teaching methods that can be employed into all three parts of the lesson plan:

1. Lecture: A speech by one speaker before an audience.

2. Group Discussion: A planned conversation among three or more persons on a selected topic – with leadership.

3. Panel Discussion: A planned conversation before an audience on a selected topic; requires three or more panelists and a leader.

4. Panel Forum: A panel followed by audience participation.

5. Buzz Groups: Small study groups discussing assigned problems – usually for the purpose of reporting back to the large group.

6. Role Playing: The unrehearsed, dramatic enactment of a human conflict situation by two or more persons for analysis by the group.

7. Case Study: An account of a problem situation, including sufficient detail to make it possible for groups to analyze problems involved.

8. Brain Storming: A method of problem solving in which group members suggest in rapid-fire order all of the possible solutions they can think of.

9. Listening Teams: Formed by dividing an audience into teams in advance of a presentation. Each team is requested to listen with specific assignments in mind, then report on their assignment.

10. Debate: A method in which speakers for and against a proposition present their points of view. Group members may question the presenters.

11. Formal Discussion: Involves stating the problems, getting the facts, considering possible solutions, and selecting best solutions.

12. Symposium: Series of short speeches before an audience – with leadership; speeches present different aspects of a topic.

13. Symposium – Forum: A symposium followed by audience participation.

14. Study Guides: A series of questions to be answered in large group, small groups, or individually.

Here are many methods you can try. Be daring and be creative when you put these into good use, and you will be surprised how your class will be infused with new energy and enthusiasm. I suggest every lesson plan should include at least three of them in an attempt to get more people involved and engaged in the lesson itself. Remember, these methods can be used in any of the three parts of the lesson.

3. Application

The third and last part of a good lesson plan is *Application*. That is, how will we apply this Bible truth to Monday morning? How will we practically and tangibly flesh it out in the real world?

A member of our church, Tony Williams, said he got a call from an usher in the church that his son had broken one of the offering plates in Sunday School. He asked his son, "Zach, why did you break the offering plate?" And his son replied, "I placed it on the ground and stood in it because I wanted to give everything I had to the Lord." That is what a good lesson should do for us. After we have been motivated to study the Scripture and examined the biblical text itself, we should come to the place of offering ourselves to the One who gave His all for us! Let's not leave the Word in the gym of intellectual exercise but rather take it into the streets of sin and despair.

All three parts of the lesson plan are necessary. They work together much like an airline flight. *Motivation* gets the plane up and running and off the ground. *Examination* charts your course and keeps you on the right path along the journey. The gauges are consistently read to monitor any danger and to keep pointing us toward the final destination. *Application* lands the plane and gets it on the ground. As in any flight, sooner or later you have to bring that baby down and land it. A good lesson will not continually circle the airport of life. It will land at its predetermined spot in the lives of people.

CORE VALUE
NUMBER THREE:

Ministering
to *People*

CHAPTER 7

The Care Group Ministry

Each Sunday morning adults come to church needing to experience three different dynamics. They need to be influenced by worship, instructed in the Word, and impacted by friends. These three needs are met by our time of worship, the Sunday School lesson, and time shared in a Care Group. Care Groups, therefore, need to be viewed as a vital part of the Sunday morning experience and not something that is optional.

Care Groups play a major role in the total Sunday morning experience for adults, but they also play a major role in the Sunday School's "work of the ministry": reaching people, teaching people, and ministering to people. Care Groups are the principal means of accomplishing the third task of Sunday School – ministering to people. By structuring our adult classes into Care Groups, we provide a mechanism to minister to people. Other plans have failed in their attempt to meet people at the point of their need because they are structured around an organization or program. Care Groups are organized and may be considered a program. However, they operate, first and foremost, on the premise of relationships.

At First Baptist Woodstock, our adult classes break into Care Groups each Sunday for twenty minutes (see *Class Structure,* chapter eight). During this time, the Care Group Leader takes the roll, so he will know who is absent and needs a contact that week. In addition, he leads the group to pray for each others' prayer requests, makes assignments for hospital or ministry visits, and makes them aware of small group discipleship opportunities.

Corrie Ten Boom once said, "The measure of a life is not its duration but its donation." Care Groups help us "donate" to each other and minister to those who are hurting. Here are nine reasons I believe ministering is so vital today.

1. Pain and hurt are part of the human experience.

"For we know that the whole creation groaneth and travaileth in pain together until now" (Romans 8:22).

When Adam and Eve introduced sin into the world, they ushered in pain and hurt. Pain comes in the form of physical hurt, but it also comes in the form of emotional hurt. Since that time in the Garden of Eden, man has been inflicted with suffering. However, I am of the opinion that as we draw closer and closer to the world's greatest time of suffering – The Great Tribulation – mankind will experience the acceleration of agony. We cannot deny the increase of murder, abortion, pornography, hatred, divorce, child abuse, drugs, violence, etc. in our society. Sin has been turned loose and is cutting a destructive path through our heartland. Because pain and suffering are at an all-time high, the need for genuine, loving ministry has never been so vital. Our sin-filled society has jeopardized our families and, consequently, our society; but it also gives the Church of Jesus Christ a tremendous opportunity to step into people's lives with the love of Christ and do vital, life-saving ministry.

2. Every believer needs the association of other believers.

"And let us consider one another to provoke unto love and to good works: Not forsaking the assembling of ourselves together, as the manner of some is; but exhorting one another: and so much the more, as ye see the day approaching" (Hebrews 10:24-25).

"So we, being many, are one body in Christ, and every one members *one of another*" (Romans 12:5, *emphasis mine*).

Dr. Ray Orland stated it well when he said, "The Christian who is not committed to a group of other believers for praying, sharing, and serving so that he is known, as he knows others, is not an obedient Christian. He is not in the will of God. However vocal he may be in his theology, he is not obeying the Lord."

3. Everyone needs encouragement to grow spiritually.

"Two are better than one; because they have a good reward for their labour. For if they fall, the one will lift up his fellow: but woe to him that is alone when he falleth; for he hath not another to help him up. Again, if two lie together, then they have heat: but how can one be warm alone? And if one prevail against him, two shall withstand him; and a threefold cord is not quickly broken" (Ecclesiastes 4:9-12).

There is no such thing as a "Lone Ranger" Christian. The Bible is clear that we need each other. If not, why the command to assemble with other Christians? Those who say they can be just as good a Christian without the association and encouragement of other believers is either deceived or a liar!

4. Everyone learns from others.

"Iron sharpeneth iron; so a man sharpeneth the countenance of his friend" (Proverbs 27:17).

I have heard people describe themselves as "self-made men." In response, I always say to myself, "I pity that poor man." I don't want to be a self-made man. I want to be a better man because of all the input I have received from others. I want to be a composite of other's deposits. Don't allow your pride to blind you from the value that others will bring to your life. To be a self-made man is to be a prideful or ignorant person.

5. It is what Jesus would have us to do.

Jesus was confronted by "a certain lawyer" who wanted to know who his neighbor was. Jesus then told the story of the Good Samaritan. He concluded this story with the following:

> "Which now of these three, thinkest thou, was neighbour unto him that fell among the thieves? And he said, He that showed mercy on him. Then said Jesus unto him, Go, *and do thou likewise*" (Luke 10:36-37, *emphasis mine*).

Jesus taught we are to minister to others – even to the point of inconveniencing ourselves. He gave us the supreme example by dying on the cross for us. The Apostle Paul illustrated Jesus as the ultimate example of thinking of others in Philippians 2.

> "Let nothing be done through strife or vainglory; but in lowliness of mind let each esteem other better than themselves. Look not every man on his own things, but every man also on the things of others" (Philippians 2:3-4).

6. There is power when we pray together.

> "And this is the confidence that we have in him, that, if we ask any thing according to his will, he heareth us: And if we know that he hear us, whatsoever we ask, we know that we have the petitions that we desired of him" (1 John 5:14-15).

The prayer ministry that goes on each week in our Care Groups may be the greatest ministry the church offers. It may exceed the sermon, the Sunday School lesson, and the choir special in ministering to the hearts of needy people. Do not underestimate the prayer ministry of your Care Groups.

7. It gives strong witness to the world.

"That they all may be one; as thou, Father, art in me, and I in thee, that they also may be one in us: that the world may believe that thou hast sent me. …I in them, and thou in me, that they may be made perfect in one; and that the world may know that thou hast sent me, and hast loved them, as thou hast loved me" (John 17:21, 23).

"A new commandment I give unto you, That ye love one another; as I have loved you, that ye also love one another. By this shall all men know that ye are my disciples, if ye have love one to another" (John 13:34-35).

Through the love we have for one another, the world will see Christ in us. Thus, our love and support to others give a strong testimony to the lost world of the love of the Lord Jesus Christ that transformed us.

8. I am responsible to other believers.

"As every man hath received the gift, even so minister the same one to another, as good stewards of the manifold grace of God" (1 Peter 4:10).

We are responsible for the spiritual welfare of others. We are to help each other and minister to each other. It is not only our privilege; it is our duty.

We are responsible for the spiritual welfare of others.

9. We need to hold each other accountable.

"Brethren, if a man be overtaken in a fault, ye which are spiritual, restore such an one in the spirit of meekness; considering thyself, lest thou also be tempted" (Galatians 6:1-2).

Who should go to a brother that is slipping? Who would even know he was slipping but those who know him and have a relationship with him? Ministry best takes place within the arena of established relationships. Because two people have a relationship, they have the right to say things to each other that no one else does. Because they have a relationship, they are able to know how to minister to one another. For example, it is the person who has loved me and prayed with me and supported me that has earned the right to contact me when I have been unfaithful to attend like I should.

Ministry best takes place within the arena of established relationships.

When you observe these nine ministry reasons, you will quickly notice all of them operate best in the confines of a small group. A mother who just found out her teenage daughter is pregnant out of wedlock may not share that in a class of twenty-five people. However, she may share that in a Care Group setting of eight people who she has met with and prayed with often. Care Groups are a great way to get people involved in each other's lives.

The "One Anothers" of Scripture

This partial list of the Bible's "one anothers" certainly helps us see God's heart for "others." A properly structured Care Group ministry is an "others" ministry. As someone has said, "Life is a lot like tennis: the one who can best serve seldom loses."

A properly structured Care Group ministry is an "others" ministry.

- Encourage One Another – "Wherefore comfort yourselves together, and edify one another, even as also ye do" (1 Thessalonians 5:11).

- Accept One Another – "Wherefore receive ye one another, as Christ also received us, to the glory of God" (Romans 15:7).

- Be Affectionate One to Another – "Be kindly affectioned one to another with brotherly love" (Romans 12:10a).

- Honor One Another – "…in honor preferring one another" (Romans 12:10b).

- Greet One Another – "Salute one another with a holy kiss. The churches of Christ salute you" (Romans 16:16).

- Serve One Another – "For, brethren, ye have been called unto liberty; only use not liberty for an occasion to the flesh, but by love serve one another" (Galatians 5:13).

- Bear One Another's Burdens – "Bear ye one another's burdens, and so fulfill the law of Christ" (Galatians 6:2).

How to Organize Care Groups

From much failure, I have learned how to organize a Sunday School class into Care Groups. Usually, a random dispersion of the saints will come back to haunt you. I recommend two ways to divide your classes into effective, functional Care Groups. First, divide and list every member of your class into one of the three groups:

- Touch Group – Those who attend up to six times a year.

- Ministry Group – Those who attend seven to twenty-three times a year.

- Core Group – Those who attend twenty-four or more times per year.

Use the following example as a model of identifying and listing class members into attendance categories.

Touch Group	Ministry Group	Core Group
Joe	Jim	Jeff
Bill	Bob	Buster
Tim	Tom	Travis
Sue	Sally	Sarah
Mary	Martha	Melanie
Ann	Angie	Anita

After you have identified each person in the class into one of the three attendance groups, then evenly disperse them into the Care Groups of six to twelve people. For effective ministry, keep the Care Groups small. Use the following illustration as a guide.

Care Group 1	Care Group 2	Care Group 3
Joe	Bill	Tim
Sue	Mary	Ann
Jim	Bob	Tom
Sally	Martha	Angie
Jeff	Buster	Travis
Sarah	Melanie	Anita

This system evenly distributes all those in the Touch Group, Ministry Group, and Core Group into the three Care Groups. Each Care Group now has the same amount of "Core" people from which to put to work; the same amount of marginal "Ministry Group" persons; and the same amount of people from the "Touch Group" who need those special touches.

It is important to know how to divide the class into Care Groups, but it is equally important to know how to cultivate these three groups of people. We must acknowledge that everyone has "X" amount of time and "X" amount of energy that can be contributed to their church duties, and both time and energy are limited resources. So it is prudent to guide Care Group Leaders in distributing their time and energy in the most efficient manner to these three groups. Here is my recommendation.

Touch Group – These people attend church about three times a year – Christmas, Easter, and if their mother attends, Mother's Day. Truth of the matter is, these people probably are not coming and will not be actively involved in your Sunday School class. However, when (not if) a tragedy occurs in their lives (divorce, loss of a loved one, child on drugs, unmarried daughter becomes pregnant, etc.), they will be more receptive to your message. We must, therefore, continue to reach out and "touch" them so that we "earn a hearing" when the crisis comes. Visit them, but do not consume a lot of visitation time on them until the crisis occurs. When the crisis does occur, move in and minister aggressively to them. Best means of contacting is by phone.

Ministry Group - If you want to see immediate results in your attendance, then this is the group on which to expend your time and energy. As you continually minister to them, you see them go from attending fifteen times a year to twenty times a year; and eventually, they move over into the Core Group. Use your personal visitation time here, and pour yourselves into these people. They are the next generation of leaders in your Sunday School.

Core Group - This is the group from which you should develop leaders to minister to the former two groups. By the time people reach this stage, they are committed enough to the church to want to become involved. It is here you need to help them fulfill their desire for meaningful service; or you will see, at best, their enthusiasm dampen; or at worse, they will leave altogether. People vote every Sunday with their attendance and their giving. By virtue of their consistent attendance, the "Core Group" people are indicating potential and/or desire for fruitful service.

A second way to divide a class into Care Groups is by age. This works well with a growing class. Consider this scenario. A class is designed for an age grade of 30-39. This class is outreach minded and experiencing growth. As they witness and invite people to Sunday School, a man in the class leads a 45-year-old work associate to Christ and enrolls him in Sunday School. At the same time, a lady in the class leads her 25-year-old neighbor to the Lord and enrolls her in Sunday School. Both of these new converts will want to attend Sunday School with their Christian friends. They have no other relationships in the church, so it would be unnatural for us to expect them to go to another class – although the age grading will now be compromised. This 30-39 year old class has now broadened to 25-45 year olds.

This ushers in the strategy of dividing Care Groups in this class by age. We might have individual Care Groups for 25-31 year olds, 32-35 year olds, 36-39 year olds, and 40-45 year olds. If the class grows, start new Care Groups within the class. Like birthing a new class, you can start a unit (Care Group) within a unit (class).

Eventually, we will birth a new class from this class. When we do, we will birth a class by taking either the oldest Care Group or the youngest Care Group and starting a new class with them. This method will allow us to reduce the expanded age of our existing class and, at the same time, start new classes within already established relationships and without creating major upheaval within the group. This process takes more time than restructuring the whole adult age division, but it is a less painful way to accomplish age grading.

I started this chapter by stating adults need to be influenced by worship, instructed in the Word, and influenced by friends. With this in mind, here is how they work together.

Worship Time	Class Time	Care Group Time
Listen to the Word	Learn from the Word	Live the Word
Exposition of the Word	Examination of the Word	Exercise the Word
We hear the Word	We discover the Word	We use the Word
Scripture is preached	Scripture is presented	Scripture is practiced
Relationships are…	Relationships are…	Relationships are…
Hand to hand	Face to face	Heart to heart

To summarize, active, functioning Care Groups will:

- Take pressure off the teacher. He can now concentrate on teaching the Bible and leading the class, according to the *Sunday School Philosophy.*

- Involve more people in ministry.

- Aid the class in doing more for others.

- Keep ministry needs from "slipping through the cracks."

- Establish an easy and a natural way to develop relationships.

CHAPTER 8

Class

Structure

The actual class time on Sunday morning needs to be structured, so we can highlight the three tasks of Sunday School: reaching people, teaching people, and ministering to people. That which gets rewarded and emphasized is what gets done. Therefore, it behooves us to structure our Sunday School time in a manner that promotes the purpose of the organization. Time is a limited resource, so we must exercise much wisdom in using it.

Time is a limited resource, so we must
exercise much wisdom in using it.

I recommend an hour and fifteen minutes each week for Sunday School. It is hard to give appropriate emphasis to the three tasks of the Sunday School in a shorter time frame. We want this time to be used wisely and to fulfill the three purposes of the Sunday School. The following usage of our class time will keep us on track to be a purpose-driven Sunday School with an intentional plan to accomplish an intentional purpose! I recommend a Sunday morning structure that follows the sequence and time allotment listed below:

1. Fellowship Time (10 minutes)

We surveyed about 350 adults that attend our Sunday School and discovered the top ingredients they loved about Sunday School were the fellowship, relationships, and "family atmosphere." Having the Fellowship Time first sets the atmosphere and engages people in a comfortable, friendly environment. This affords the rest of the class time to be placed in an environment conducive for warmth, interaction, and a good experience. By setting the Fellowship Time first, it promotes people being on time and it also prevents latecomers from missing the Bible study, Care Group time, and the outreach emphasis time.

2. Announcements (5 minutes)

Sunday School must become the "Communication Center" of the church which is especially true of growing churches. No longer can the pastor get up and make an abundance of announcements in the worship service or make pleas for additional help in various ministries within the church. Sunday School is the place for these announcements. Caution: Plan and coordinate your announcements. People can take in only so much at one time. Too many announcements and promotions dilute each other to the point that nothing really gets emphasized. In addition, too many announcements become deflating to class morale.

3. Outreach Discussion/Testimonies/Emphasis (10 Minutes)

Each week the class Outreach Leader should have a few minutes to promote evangelism. If Sunday School is to be the outreach arm of the church, then evangelism must get some "air time" on Sunday morning. If the number-one purpose of the Sunday School is to reach people, then we must keep it in front of the people each and every week.

This is an excellent time for the Outreach Leader to distribute visitation assignments to those who are not able to make the weekly visitation night. The Outreach Leader also can retrieve assignments distributed the week before. This also is a great time to have a soul-winning testimony or to introduce a visitor who is attending due to the contacts made by the class.

4. Care Group Time (20 Minutes)

Each week the Care Group Leaders of the class have an opportunity to meet with their Care Group. During this time, they will take the roll and then assign absentee contacts to other Care Group members to make the following week. They will discuss ministry needs of those in the Care Group and organize the people to meet those needs. Then they will share prayer concerns and pray for each other. This is a tall order for a twenty-minute session, so the Care Group ministry needs to become a well-oiled machine.

The Care Groups can meet in circles in the four corners of the room and even some in the middle, depending on the room size. We have some Care Groups that actually go into the hall or even outside if the weather cooperates.

5. Bible Study (30 Minutes)

The teacher should have at least thirty minutes for the lesson. If announcements are short, he can absorb a little more time. I am a teacher at heart and personally want more than thirty minutes. However, we must give emphasis to all three tasks of the Sunday School during class time. We must admit we cannot give people all the Word they need in thirty minutes but then neither could we if we had an hour. We must depend on the pastor's sermons, discipleship groups, and their personal Bible study to supplement the Bible lesson they receive in Sunday School.

It must be pointed out that the Word of God is preeminent and the Bible Study time should not be consumed in needless talk about ball games, business, etc. The Word of God transforms lives. The Apostle Paul instructed the church at Rome: "So then faith cometh by hearing, and hearing by the word of God" (Romans 10:17). The only way we can increase the faith of our class members and disciple them into Christlikeness is through the infallible Word of God!

Platforms

I am big on platforms. By that, I mean if something is important, then it should be given a "platform" to promote itself. For example, we would all say winning lost people to Jesus is the purpose of the church (and Sunday School). However, we never give it any "prime time." We say it is important, and yet we never promote it. We say meeting people's needs is biblically incumbent upon us all. Yet we never put together a plan to do this. It really is true that when everything is said and done, more is said than done! We have got to cut that out. We must start putting feet to our beliefs.

If something is important, then it should be given a "platform" to promote itself.

This class structure incorporates all three tasks of the Sunday School into the Sunday morning experience:

Task 1: Reach People. This is promoted during the ten minutes when the Outreach Leader shares a testimony, introduces new people attending the class because a class outreach team visited them, distributes visits and contacts to be made during the week, and receives reports from those who were given assignments the week before.

Task 2: Teach People. A lesson from God's Word is presented by the teacher or the assistant teacher that will instruct people in godly living. This time is extremely valuable. Because the Word of God disciples people, Sunday School is the greatest discipleship training program a church has! We do not have the power or ability to change people, but the Word of God does. We need to be faithful to unleash its power every Lord's day.

Task 3: Minister to People. Our Care Group time affords us the opportunity to touch people, to minister to them, to pray for them, and to lift them up.

As you can see, this class structure helps your Sunday School to be intentional and to focus on the objectives of the organization. Obviously, there will be some weeks that special things are going on that require some deviation from this format. The format is not a legalistic guideline that cannot be altered. Instead it is a compass to keep us pressing toward our destination.

This class structure helps your Sunday School to be intentional and to focus on the objectives of the organization.

Tips for Using Scheduled Class Time

Using Class Outreach Time (10 minutes)

Basic:

- Discuss overall Sunday School strategy (Great Commission).

- Discuss what outreach means to and for your class specifically.

- Pray in class about the need for the class to become Great Commission oriented.

- Pray for God to lead a class member to become the class Outreach Leader.

- Ask class members to identify lost family members, friends, co-workers, and neighbors.

- Pray for these lost people by name.

- Discuss ways God could use your class to reach prospects and absentees.

- Have a Visitation Team from your class participating each week at churchwide visitation.

Intermediate:

- Continue basic practices listed above.

- Allow the Outreach Leader to lead Outreach Emphasis time each Sunday in class.

- Distribute prospects to class members from the class prospect book, so they can contact them.

- Identify prospects from class members.

- Discuss ways to reach these prospects and pray for them.

- Plan class fellowships and outings where prospects can be invited.

- Ask class members to call, write, and visit prospects.

- Enlist a Visitation Team from your class who will visit together and participate in soul-winning training.

- Allow members to share a testimony about a witnessing experience.

- Pray for the class Outreach Leader and Visitation Team.

Advanced:

- Continue the basic and intermediate practices as listed above.

- Follow the church's Sunday School strategy and structure.

- Enlist more class members in soul-winning training.

- Pray for more laborers to go into the harvest fields.

Using Class Care Group Time (20 minutes)

Basic:

- Discuss overall Sunday School strategy (Great Commission).

- Teach members how to have a quiet time.

- Inform them about upcoming Discipleship Training classes.

- Pray about the need for the class to become Great Commission oriented.

- Pray for God to raise up Care Group Leaders.

- Allow Care Groups to meet before the Bible study lesson.

- Direct class members to identify ministry needs within the group.

- Pray for each other in the group.

Intermediate:

- Continue basic practices listed above.

- Allow Care Group Leaders to meet with their Care Group as prescribed in the Class Time Structure.

- Identify absentees in the Care Group time.

- Pray for absentees during the Care Group time.

- Assign an absentee to group members to contact that week.

- Identify critical ministry needs within the group, and plan a strategy to meet those needs immediately.

Advanced:

- Continue the basic and intermediate practices listed above.

- Lead group members to participate in weekly visitation for the purpose of visiting absentee members.

- Lead the Care Group to be the seed members to start a new Sunday School class.

- Organize the class into Care Groups, according to the recommended strategy (see chapter seven on *The Care Group Ministry*).

CORE VALUE
NUMBER FOUR:

Involving
People

CHAPTER 9

Involvement: The Pathway to Success

Over and over again, I remind my Education Staff of this principle: The secret to success is the involvement of people. This is true with the Little League baseball organization, the PTA, the civic club, politics; and it is certainly true of Sunday School. Sunday School puts more people to work in the church than any other ministry. It gets more people involved in ministry than any other organization or program. Sunday School is the most practical way I know to fulfill Ephesians 4:11-12:

> "And he (Jesus) gave some, apostles; and some, prophets; and some, evangelists; and some, pastors and teachers; For the perfecting of the saints, for the work of the ministry, for the edifying of the body of Christ."

The secret to success is the involvement of people.

This passage instructs "pastors and teachers" to equip the saints to do ministry, to get people trained and involved in helping and growing others. It is then, and only then, the church will experience numerical and spiritual growth.

I had the privilege of leading a three-day conference in the Ukraine for 400 pastors. During that time, I taught them about their need to start small groups. In most of their churches, they only have a worship service. Therefore, only two people are busy doing ministry: the pastor and worship leader. I tried to help them understand the need for small groups and the vitality it would bring to their churches when the saints got busy doing ministry. At the end of each session, I would have them say with me: "The secret to success is the involvement of people." They really took to this, and it became a fun and delightful time for them.

I must confess I am amazed at churches that want to eliminate Sunday School. I must ask:

- Is there another ministry that gets people involved like Sunday School?

- Is there a better mechanism in a local church to mobilize people for evangelism?

- Is there a better way to minister to people?

- Is there a better way to place people in an environment for relationship building?

- Is there a better way to teach people the Word of God?

- Is there a better way to assimilate new believers?

I must confess I have not found anything that effectively incorporates the Great Commission in tangible, practical ways better than Sunday School. Many have become skeptics of Sunday School when I believe many should champion her cause. Sunday School encourages Jesus' teaching about servanthood:

"But Jesus called them to him, and saith unto them, Ye know that they which are accounted to rule over the Gentiles exercise lordship over them; and their great ones exercise authority upon them. But so shall it not be among you: but whosoever will be great among you, shall be your minister: And whosoever of you will be the chiefest, shall be servant of all. For even the Son of man came not to be ministered unto, but to minister, and to give his life a ransom for many" (Mark 10:42-45).

I have not found anything that effectively incorporates the Great Commission in tangible, practical ways better than Sunday School.

Jesus promoted serving and ministering to others; Sunday School promotes serving and ministering to others. We practice servanthood when we teach, witness to unbelievers, visit the hospital, provide food for those who have lost a loved one, etc. Sunday School involves people as teachers, outreach leaders, care group leaders, fellowship leaders, department directors, secretaries, greeters, and administrators. Sunday School must minister to newborns, senior adults, and everyone in between. Forgive the redundancy, but Sunday School involves people in vital ministry that makes an eternal difference in the lives of those whom Jesus loves.

Sunday School involves people in vital ministry that makes an eternal difference in the lives of those whom Jesus loves.

So the question we must ask is: Do we have enough people in ministry? I do not know of a church that has all of the Sunday School workers it needs, and this is good. If you have all you need, then your organization is too small and is in desperate need of expansion.

I recently talked with a staff member in a growing church who was concerned about the lack of growth in the choir. This church has two services, and the same choir sings at both of them. The choir loft is full at both services. Their problem is a lack of expansion. They want the choir loft to be full for their two morning worship hours. However, by using the same people at both services, they leave no room for others to see the opportunity or sense the need to join.

Churches that need to implement a second Sunday School hour are usually fearful they will not be able to fill all of the needed positions for such an undertaking. My question is: Do you have all of your positions filled currently? Usually, I get a negative response. My next question is: Do you have to fill all of your current vacancies before you go to the second Sunday School hour? If you do, you will never go to dual Sunday Schools because you will never fill all of your positions. So if you are going to have some unfilled positions, you might as well do it with two Sunday Schools as one. Fact of the matter is, you will never fill all of your positions – regardless of how many Sunday Schools you have. This being the case, my last question is: So what are you waiting for?

The adult division is the key to getting more people involved in ministry through the Sunday School, and the adult teachers are the key persons. Without their buy-in, the church will be hard pressed to see the expansion of their Sunday School ministry and the involvement of more people. Many adult teachers do not want their class members to leave to serve in another area. They have worked hard to build their class, grow their class, and disciple others. Like a child leaving home, it pains the teacher to release those into whom he has poured his life. Let's explore two scenarios and analyze them for a proper perspective on involving others in ministry.

Scenario 1 - The Minister of Education asks an adult teacher if he can make a plea for some to leave the class to work in the Preschool, Children's, and Youth departments. The teacher is upset with the request and says he does not want to do that. Upon further discussion, the Minister of Education discovers this teacher has worked hard to grow his class and finally has reached twenty-three in average attendance. He is very pleased with this growth and does not want to "start all over again" with a few. But what he fails to see is the need in the younger departments and the impossibility of those departments to raise up leadership from their own constituency. Furthermore, his class will eventually suffer if the younger areas falter.

Scenario 2 – The Sunday School Director suggests to an adult teacher: "I have been noticing Bob. He has grown in the Lord so much and last week substitute taught in another class and did a marvelous job. I want to use him as a new teacher, bring a few members out of your class to join him, and start a new class with them." The teacher often becomes dejected and offers, "Don't take Bob. He's the best one I got." Well, did the teacher expect the Sunday School Director to take his worst one?

Let me address both of these scenarios by using a personal illustration. My oldest child Kelly was just about ready to graduate from college. With my blessing, she had been dating Ben, a fine Christian young man from our church, for some time. One Friday afternoon, Ben called the house and asked if he could come over the next morning and talk with me. We agreed on a time and concluded our brief conversation. After hanging up the phone, Linda, my wife, asked who called and I told her it was Ben. She then asked what he wanted; and I replied, "He wants to come over tomorrow morning and ask us for Kelly's hand in marriage" (I can read faster than he can write!). Sure enough, the next morning Ben came over and asked our blessing on his proposal of marriage to Kelly. We gave him our blessing and off he went.

I must confess that between Ben's call Friday afternoon and our meeting the next day a lot of things went through my mind. Kelly has been a wonderful daughter, an exemplary Christian, and a joy to her mom and I. I didn't want to see her leave. Linda and I had poured much love, time, energy, and money into our beloved daughter. Yet I always knew this moment was coming. From the time she was a little girl, I saw this day; and each time I attended a wedding, I fought back the tears when the father walked down the aisle with his precious daughter and then gave her away. I knew my time was coming.

So when Ben came over that morning, I had mixed emotions. When Ben asked for my blessing, I told him this was a bittersweet moment. It was bitter in that I did not look forward to Kelly leaving our home. It was sweet in that we could not have found a better husband for Kelly than Ben. Also this is the natural, normal cycle of life. The day had come for Kelly to stand on her own two feet and be a responsible, mature adult. If she were incapable of doing that, then we would have done a poor job raising her.

Between Ben's call Friday afternoon and our meeting Saturday morning, one other thing kept coming to my mind. When Kelly was a little girl, Linda and I joined some other young parents at our church and watched some films by Dr. James Dobson. In one of those films, Dr. Dobson said your children are not yours; they are ultimately God's. They are on loan to us from God. He went on to say God has entrusted us with this child to love and raise "in the nurture and admonition of the Lord" (Ephesians 6:4). Then the day will come that you have to give the child back to God. Dr. Dobson then admonished us to rear our children so that we will be pleased with the finished product when we give them back to God.

So it is with every adult teacher. Their class members are not theirs; they are God's. They are just on loan from God for a period of time. God has entrusted the teacher with the responsibility of caring for their souls and feeding them spiritually, so they can grow up to be big boys and girls in Christ. God never intended for them to sit in a class all of their lives and never experience the joy and fulfillment of getting out on their own and standing on their own two spiritual feet. If they are incapable of service, then the teacher cannot consider his ministry to these people a complete success. You see, a teacher's job is not done by getting people to attend and seeing spiritual maturity in their lives. His job is complete when he has discipled people to the point that they understand the purpose in their own service and then seek a place to minister.

His job is complete when he has discipled people to the point that they understand the purpose in their own service and then seek a place to minister.

Adult classes are the key to supplying workers throughout the Sunday School and other ministries within the church. Adult teachers are the key persons in making this a reality. I cannot overstate the importance of every adult teacher understanding this concept. If they do, your church will not be a stagnant church; she will be in a constant building program!

In addition to needing teachers who multiply themselves, we need those who are willing to be trailblazers—those who will take a few "seed members" and strike out on an adventure of reaching those who are unrelated to Christ and/or the church. Many will take over an existing class. They will trod the path that has been previously paved by others. A few brave souls will blaze the trail for others to follow. The Apostle Paul was such:

> "Yea, so have I strived to preach the gospel, not where Christ was named, lest I should build upon another man's foundation" (Romans 15:20).

Paul understood the need to reproduce himself and to "franchise" the church. Every fast-food restaurant in America understands the way to grow their business by constantly franchising. The church has the greatest franchise on God's green earth, and yet we keep it to ourselves. Let's look at three basic questions to help us understand the necessity of creating new classes and franchising the ministry of reaching, teaching, and ministering to people.

Why?

We need to help people catch the philosophy and purpose involved in birthing new classes. Those who do not understand will naturally resist this concept. They often will question whether it will make a difference. It will make a difference because it provides opportunities for others to become active in exercising their spiritual gifts. We have many whose gifts and abilities lie dormant. We must discover those gifts and put them into service within the body of Christ. God did not intend for His children to waste their gifts, and He certainly did not intend for the church to deny people opportunities to employ their giftedness. Paul spent three chapters (1 Corinthians 12-14) instructing the church at Corinth concerning spiritual gifts. He did not want them to be ignorant in this matter:

We need to help people catch the philosophy and purpose involved in birthing new classes.

"Now concerning spiritual gifts, brethren, I would not have you ignorant" (1 Corinthians 12:1).

Paul wanted every member employing every gift, so the body of Christ could operate the way God intended.

"From whom the whole body fitly joined together and compacted by that which *every joint supplieth*, according to the effectual working in the measure of *every part*, maketh increase of the body unto the edifying of itself in love" (Ephesians 4:16, *emphasis mine*).

Another concern that is raised the most is the issue of breaking up fellowship. We tell people to get in Sunday School, so they can build relationships; and then we ask them to leave those relationships to start new works. It sounds so confusing and many times leads to frustration with many of the saints. So how do we address this legitimate concern? I think we turn to the Scriptures.

"That which we have seen and heard declare we unto you, that ye also may have fellowship with us: and truly our fellowship is with the Father, and with his Son Jesus Christ" (1 John 1:3).

According to the Apostle John, our fellowship with each other is predicated first on our fellowship with God the Father and Son. If we are in tune with God and He desires for others to get involved using their spiritual gifts in ministering to others, then our fellowship with each other only will be enhanced because we are walking in God's will. This being the case, fellowship will increase, not decrease. Furthermore, if new people are brought into the kingdom, then our fellowship grows because it incorporates more believers.

I wonder if the family, friends, and acquaintances of the disciples complained to Jesus because He broke up their fellowship when He called them to follow Him? I wonder if the church at Antioch fussed when the Holy Ghost said, "Separate me Barnabas and Saul for the work whereunto I have called them" (Acts 13:2)? I am sure they had sweet *koinonia* with those two spiritual giants, but we know from Acts 13:3 the Antioch Christians did not murmur and complain:

> "And when they had fasted and prayed, and laid their hands on them, they sent them away."

The leader must know this will help accomplish the Great Commission and the tasks of Sunday School. Here are five observations of which to be aware:

1. Most people do not buy in to birthing a new unit out of their class because they do not understand the reason for doing it.

Educate your people concerning this. Take the time to invest in their progress of this concept. Make sure you instruct them as to the whys as well as the hows. Most will need to process this over a period of time. Do not be naïve and expect everyone to jump on board the first time you share this. New ideas are rarely ever embraced at first. Time, patience, love, and instruction will usually water the seed of a new thought.

2. New Units = New People = New Growth

As a general rule, new classes grow at a much better rate than do classes that have tenure. I think my "Lego Principle" will explain the reason for this. When my son Jake was a young boy, we bought him a set of Legos. He loved to connect them together by using their "snap-on points." He would build all kinds of things and occupy himself for hours with those Legos. I noticed those individual Legos were like people in the church. They came in all kind of sizes, shapes, and colors. And each Lego had a certain amount of snap-on points: some had two snap-on points; others had four, six, eight, and some as many as twelve.

Like Legos, everyone who comes to Sunday School has "X" amount of snap-on points. These snap-on points represent the time, energy, and money each individual has to give to the church. These are the only three things a person can give to the church, and each one is a limited resource. The dilemma occurs the longer an individual is in the church because more and more of his snap-on points are taken up. He has a few snap-on points taken up with several different relationships—maybe in the choir or with a committee responsibility. Before long, all of his snap-on points are taken up with none left for anything else. Then a new member joins his Sunday School class and needs to snap-on to others in the class. The new member has all of his snap-on points to give away, but this poor soul has none left with which to attach to the new member. The new member may get disgruntled and leave the class or church altogether and consider people there unfriendly when, in reality, the class is full of long-tenured members who have no available resource left to give away.

This is the main reason new classes reach new people better than long-tenured classes. In addition, the new class may be more hungry and aggressive and less satisfied than a class that has already made its mark within the church.

3. Most classes reach a saturation point at between eighteen-to twenty-four months.

Somewhere around the eighteen-to twenty-four-month time frame, a person's Legos are completely consumed. For this reason, a class that has been together for two years or longer runs the risk of stymied growth. At this point, the class becomes maintenance-driven instead of mission-driven. At this juncture, the class needs to start a new class by raising up a new teacher with some seed members. The beauty of this is that it helps both the long-tenured class and the new class. The people who make up the new class are now freed from the snap-on points that were consumed by their former class. With their released snap-on points, they can now connect with others whom they are trying to reach. The long-tenured class also has been released from some snap-on points that were taken up by those who left to start the new work. Therefore, both groups are now positioned for new growth. For these reasons, every adult class should start a new class at least every two years.

4. We must constantly remind ourselves that church is not just for us.

We must grasp the vision of the Great Commission. Jesus never intended for church to be just for us. He wants all men to come to Him.

"For God so loved the world, that he gave his only begotten Son, that whosoever believeth in him should not perish, but have everlasting life" (John 3:16).

"Who will have all men to be saved, and to come unto the knowledge of the truth" (1 Timothy 2:4).

"The Lord is not slack concerning his promise, as some men count slackness; but is longsuffering to us-ward, not willing that any should perish, but that all should come to repentance" (2 Peter 3:9).

Why are we in the church? We are here for those who are not yet here.

"Go ye therefore, and teach all nations, baptizing them in the name of the Father, and of the Son, and of the Holy Ghost: Teaching them to observe all things whatsoever I have commanded you: and, lo, I am with you always, even unto the end of the world. Amen" (Matthew 28:19-20).

"And the lord said unto the servant, Go out into the highways and hedges, and compel them to come in, that my house may be filled" (Luke 14:23).

5. We must understand it is God's will for the church to grow.

Does God intend for individual Christians to grow? Yes. Does God intend for the church to grow? Yes. Then is it not consistent to say God intends for Sunday School classes to grow? Yes!

Is it God's will for Christians to reproduce themselves and make believers out of others? Yes. Is it God's will for churches to reproduce themselves and start new mission churches? Yes. Then is it not consistent to believe God intends for Sunday School classes to reproduce themselves as well? Yes!

It is evident that logic is on the side of starting new classes, involving more people, and doing more ministry. Classes should take pride in the fact they have given birth to daughter classes. These daughter classes can still join them for fellowships and special projects.

Buddy Hulsey is a teacher in our church. His class has started many classes over the many years of his teaching and leadership. His class has mothered many daughter classes. These daughter classes have now given birth to daughter classes that have given birth to other classes that have given birth to more classes. His class is now a great-great-grandparent and is responsible for much of our Sunday School growth.

When?

This deals with timing. It is important to start classes at the right time. Here are five questions that will assist in directing the process.

1. Is it the right time of year?

It is ill-advised to start a new class during the summer months or the weeks leading up to it. It is deflating to start a class in a season when the attendance will be low. It is generally good to start the new class during a high attendance campaign. The new class can take advantage of this and start on a high note. Whenever you start a class, plan to implement it when the tide is coming in, not going out.

2. Have we reached a saturation point?

If a class has been plateaued, it may be time for it to mother a class. This may be an indication the class has no more snap-on points remaining. So often we allow classes to just exist in a plateaued state instead of initiating a plan of action that can move them off dead center.

You may remember from the Scriptures that four lepers were going to die of starvation. So they went into the camp of the Syrians—only to find the Lord had scared the Syrians off with "a noise of chariots, and a noise of horses, even the noise of a great host" (2 Kings 7:6). The four lepers then took spoil of their camp because the Syrians left in haste to preserve their lives. Then the lepers reported this news to the king, so the whole nation could benefit from their good tidings. The question that spurred the lepers to action was: "Why sit we here until we die?" (2 Kings 7:3). I think that question is pertinent for our day. Why do we sit idly by while our Sunday School classes are experiencing famine and just biding time until death takes its prey? When a class has reached a saturation point, it is time to send out the lepers and let them discover new camps that the Lord has prepared for us.

Why do we sit idly by while our Sunday School classes are experiencing famine and just biding time until death takes its prey?

3. Does a class leader know every person by name?

Often I am asked, "Allan, when is a class too big?" That question desires a numerical answer. However, I am not comfortable answering numerically. Let me respond as Jesus often did – with another question: When is a church too big? Should we set a standard that churches grow to 500 in attendance and then have to start a mission church? We allow the church to experience growth again; but when they reach the magical number of 500, they have to start another daughter church. Most would say, "That is preposterous!" I would agree. Every church has a potential that is different from other churches, and every pastor has his unique leadership abilities. So it is with Sunday School classes and teachers. Why do we have one standard for churches and an entirely different standard for classes? We must avoid the "cookie cutter" approach with people, classes, and churches. God never meant for us to be a replica of each other.

Jesus gave us a good principle in teaching the parable of the talents. I believe we have some "five-talent teachers," some "two-talent teachers," and some "one-talent teachers." It is my desire to accommodate all of these teachers and support each of them and their ability to grow their class. This knowledge will help me aid each of these leaders with a proper perspective and expectation level. It also will guide me in knowing when to initiate a new class start from their group. As a side note, this greatly benefits me when I design new educational facilities or renovation projects. I must be able to house all three types of teachers. I do not want to put a "five-talent teacher" in a "one-talent room." Neither do I want to discourage my "one-talent teacher" by placing him in a room he cannot fill. Neither of the three is more special than the others—no more than one pastor is more special than another. The issue is not giftedness but obedience. If a "one-talent teacher" is producing "one-talent fruit," then he is "successful." If a "five-talent teacher" is producing "four-talent fruit," then he is not accomplishing the "good works, which God hath before ordained that we should walk in them" (Ephesians 2:10). Jesus said, "For unto whomsoever much is given, of him shall be much required" (Luke 12:48).

Back to the question: "Allan, when is a class too big?" My answer: "When the teacher or Care Group Leaders don't know every person on roll by name." Sunday School is a place to go where people know your name. Sunday School is not an age-graded worship service—like so many have become. This means only a few people are involved, and everyone else just "sits and soaks." Sunday School involves people in each other's lives. Sunday School, therefore, must be personal, intimate, and interactive. Even a "five-talent class" can experience this by having many Care Groups. The "five-talent class" has units (Care Groups) within a unit (class). This way relationships, participation, and involvement are maintained. But if a class grows to the point that people are not known and responsible for one another, then the class has gotten too big and grown past its ability to manage.

Sunday School is a place to go
where people know your name.

We cannot, we must not allow people to become a number instead of a name. The Anti-Christ is interested in people as numbers:

"And he causeth all, both small and great, rich and poor, free and bond, to receive a mark in their right hand, or in their foreheads: And that no man might buy or sell, save he that had the mark, or the name of the beast, or the *number* of his name" (Revelation 13:16-17, *emphasis mine*).

To the Anti-Christ, you are just a number. He is not interested in you personally; he is just interested in you joining the number he establishes in his attempt to steal glory from God.

Christ, on the other hand, is interested in you as a person. He does not give you a number but writes your name "in the Lamb's book of life" (Revelation 21:27). To Jesus, you are a name, a precious soul:

"Verily, verily, I say unto you, He that entereth not by the door into the sheepfold, but climbeth up some other way, the same is a thief and a robber. But he that entereth in by the door is the shepherd of the sheep. To him the porter openeth; and the sheep hear his voice: and he calleth his own sheep by *name*, and leadeth them out" (John 10:1-3, *emphasis mine*).

If we are to continue the ministry of Jesus, we must know our sheep by name. Every class should strive to have her leaders know every little lamb by name.

4. Have we developed new leaders for the class?

As described in the Sunday School Philosophy, the key to starting new units is developing leadership. We all take for granted that no leader can be completely trained for the task before him or her. Experience and the "school of hard knocks" cannot be factored out of the learning, developing process. It is our duty, however, to equip our soldiers for battle as best we can. Bobby Welch, pastor of the great First Baptist Church, Daytona Beach, Florida, has introduced many of us to General William Boykin, commander of the Army's Delta Force. General Boykin conveyed how the commanding officer had to identify any of his dead soldiers by acknowledging that the toe tag matched the correct body. The general said as he would stare into that cold, gray, dead face, he would ask himself the question: "Did I train this soldier to survive?"

For those of us commanding an army of soldiers for spiritual battle, we too must ask ourselves that question of every soldier that does not make it. We need a more sober, serious approach to training. We should understand that our leaders will be thrown into a heated battle. Like military soldiers, they need boot camp; they need to be equipped. To do less is to one day zip open a body bag and match a toe tag with a dead face!

5. Have we discovered new prospects for the daughter class?

Each new class should be provided with a list of church prospects. As a general rule, new classes have more fervor for outreach in their early stages than they will later on. The wise leader needs to capitalize on this. This also will start the class off with an outreach mentality that will hopefully grow into a class tradition. It provides a great platform to communicate an established expectation.

> "I have planted, Apollos watered; but God gave the increase. ...Now he
> that planteth and he that watereth are one: and every man shall receive
> his own reward according to his own labour. For we are laborers together
> with God..." (1 Corinthians 3:6, 8-9).

In this passage Paul established three principles in co-laboring with others in God's harvest fields. First, everyone builds from foundations laid by others. The ministry I have at First Baptist Church Woodstock is built upon those who preceded me. I likewise laid some foundations at the two churches I served before coming to First Baptist Church

Woodstock that others are hopefully building upon.

Secondly, the one who plants shares in the increase with the one who waters. Mother classes will share in the heavenly reward with the daughter classes of all they accomplish in Jesus' Name. The one who sows the gospel seed in the heart of an unbeliever will share in the reward with the one who eventually harvested the soul.

Lastly, when someone plants and someone waters, God gives an increase. He rewards our faithful obedience with "fruit that remains."

How?

This deals with methods. I have mentioned some before, but here are six ways to initiate the birth of new classes.

1. Birthing

Birthing involves developing new leaders from an existing class, giving them a few "seed members," and encouraging others to join them at a predetermined date. This will necessitate the teacher mentoring a teacher in training from his class and developing him to be the teacher of the new daughter class. The teacher will need to let him teach at least once a month for a time so that the class will have an opportunity to hear him and ascribe to his teaching and leadership style. People go to a certain class for the same reason they worship at a particular church – they like the preacher and they like the teacher. If the substitute teacher never gets a platform with the class, then they will not gravitate to him. He must have a forum with which to win them over. This demands a teacher who is secure and committed to reproducing himself in others.

2. Trailblazing

This method has the current teacher leaving with a few "seed members" and starting the new work while leaving the existing class with the substitute teacher in training. This puts both the new class and the existing class on new turf and requires them to blaze a new trail. I suggest the best situation in which to implement this method is when the existing teacher starts his new class at another Sunday School hour to prevent competition between the two classes and/or two teachers.

3. Contracting

Contracting establishes a predetermined number for a class to reach and then it starts a new class. One suggestion: Also include a date in case the class does not reach the predetermined number.

4. Reorganization

Reorganization means the entire adult enrollment is profiled and placed into the appropriate age-graded class. Basically, you are reshuffling the whole deck of cards. Oftentimes you must have a U-haul ready if you do this. But it is a viable and valid way to get your age-grading back on track and to start new units in the process. This method requires much more time and planning because you are corporately dealing with every class at one time; whereas the other methods are implemented to each class individually. Make sure you have the unwavering commitment from your pastor and leadership team before striking out. If not, you will strike out!

5. Relationally

As previously mentioned, this method is used with classes whose Care Groups are organized by age. A new class is started by taking either the oldest or youngest Care Group and birthing a class with them. This helps to maintain an age-graded Sunday School without reorganizing. The beauty of this method is it prevents the intrusion of already established relationships. The Care Group that starts the new unit has camaraderie and a history.

6. Topically

New units can develop around a subject of interest. We started a class for single moms and devoted the first quarter to a curriculum designed especially for this topic. Many women came who were not in Sunday School. A few weeks before the quarter ended, we offered to keep the ladies together and have them become a permanent Sunday School class. They were delighted with the suggestion. We do, however, expect any new class that initiates around a topical study to transition to regular, ongoing curriculum after the initial quarter. We believe a "balanced diet" of the Word of God is the most beneficial in producing well-rounded disciples.

We have used this same strategy in starting a class called "First Aid" for women who are "unequally yoked" in their marriages. Some of these women have seen their husbands come to faith in Christ. We start two new classes each year from our "Nearlywed" class (for engaged couples) and two from our "Newlywed" class. We have started many new classes from our seven-week New Members Class. While they are in the New Members Class, we have a new teacher come in with them, get to know them, visit them, and then start a new class with them at the conclusion of the course. These new members have all of their snap-on points to give away, so we let them give them to each other.

Five Barriers to Starting New Classes

There is probably an inexhaustible list of barriers to franchising our Sunday School, but I want to identify five of them. These barriers are comprised of ninety-percent attitude and ten-percent ability.

1. The focus of the class is turned inward

This represents a class whose mindset is to think of themselves. They have no passion for the lost or the Great Commission. They have failed to see the clear heart of God for the lost in their Bible studies. They are modern-day Pharisees who think everything revolves around them and what they think and want. They have no vision.

2. An unwillingness to pay the price.

The basic difference between a growing class and a stagnant class is the attitude of paying the price for growth. Growth is not cheap; it will exact a tiresome toil and leave you weary. However, as expensive as growth is, it is still cheaper than no growth! The difference between a growing Christian, church, and/or class and a non-growing Christian, church, and/or class is the willingness to pay the price. We only have one life to live for Christ; let us exhaust ourselves for His glory!

The basic difference between a growing class and a stagnant class is the attitude of paying the price for growth.

3. Inappropriate leadership.

Many classes do not involve more people in ministry and birth new units because they have not been led to do so. I have found a lack of leadership in this area to be most prevalent in our churches. Sheep need a shepherd; churches need leaders. Many churches are not dead; they are dormant. They need a shepherd who knows where the green pastures are.

4. Possessing a hiker's attitude rather than a trailblazer's attitude.

We must journey the road less traveled. We must have some Pauls who will forge the way for others to follow. The church has been hiking for years. It is time we took some more territory for the kingdom's sake.

5. Over-attachment to one teacher, one class, or room.

Many of us are just stuck in the same old church rut. Hey, God has got a great, big world out there. Why don't you get out and see a little of it!

"According to the grace of God which is given unto me, as a wise masterbuilder, I have laid the foundation, and another buildeth thereon..." (1 Corinthians 3:10).

CORE VALUE
NUMBER FIVE:

Assimilating *People*

CHAPTER 10

Absorbing People into the Church

Webster's Dictionary defines the word *assimilate* as: "absorb into the system." If the church is to assimilate new people, we must absorb them into the system of Christianity. We receive them; incorporate them; and through a process of time and discipleship, see them change by the transforming work of the Holy Spirit to become more like Jesus. As a newborn baby must be absorbed into the system of a home, a school, and a society, so a new believer must be brought into the ways of Christ.

Several years ago, Linda and I went on our first mission trip. We were ministering in Romania and were to be gone for a total of ten days. Our greatest concern was not the visa, passport, or even our seat assignment on a nine-hour flight. Our greatest concern was the care of our three children while we were gone. We were fortunate that a dear Christian friend, Stacie Kersey, stayed with and cared for our children. As a godly, conscientious Christian lady, Stacie had our complete trust. While meditating on this, I realized I had great concern for my children and yet the Bible calls me an "evil" father. (Luke 11:13) This truth made me keenly aware of how important it is to our perfect Heavenly Father that we go to great lengths to care for His children. His perfect love demands the best for them. This realization brings an extreme seriousness to the assimilating arm of the church – the Sunday

School. Sunday School is the ministry that shoulders the assimilation and care of God's precious children.

It is apparent that we have a fully age-graded Sunday School – a place for any person to fit who attends on Sunday morning. To not provide for one age division is to stifle the other areas because each age division is dependent upon the others. The young adult department and the preschool department lean on each other because young adults bring babies and toddlers to church with them. Likewise, the median adult department and the youth departments are inseparably linked. Inefficiency in either area can damage the other.

We must then provide a well-rounded Sunday School program for all ages. The church must have "pockets" to fit people in. I once purchased a pair of pants with no back pockets. I soon learned what a mistake that was because I always carry my wallet in my back left pocket and my handkerchief in my back right pocket. I was now forced to assimilate them into my front two pockets that were occupied with other things. My front pockets bulged to the point of discomfort and unattractiveness. After the second time I wore them, I gave them to my wife and told her to give them to someone who needed them because I didn't. My problem was the same as some Sunday Schools: we just don't provide enough pockets with which to assimilate.

There have been numerous attempts to divide people in a manner appropriate for small group Bible study. The goal is to place everyone in a homogeneous setting. Some churches assimilate adults by the age of their children since parents' lifestyles are altered by their children's stage of life. This can be complicated if parents have more than one child and further complicated if the children are separated by wide age spans. It is my conviction that age-grading is still the best way to divvy up people. There are other ways, but this method has been time-tested over many decades. Now you could divide people by weight, bank account, or their intelligence quotient; but these may expose your mortality sooner than you desire!

Biblical Assimilation

I want to walk you through a "process of absorbing" others into the church and Christlikeness. I will do this by using more definitions from *Webster's Dictionary* which further defines the word *assimilate*. But first, I want to stretch your thinking about what assimilation truly is. I want to make sure we have a biblical concept of assimilation and not merely a cultural concept. I believe God's view of assimilation leaves ours with much to be desired.

Many churches (and church leaders) determine the success of assimilating new people into the congregation based on baptisms alone. Certainly, baptism is vital because it is the outward show of an inward work of grace. This is the first step toward assimilating a newly converted believer. Others carry assimilation to another level by insisting people are not truly assimilated until they are baptized and attending regularly. The value of faithful church attendance cannot be underestimated. Without it, a new believer stands no chance of becoming all Christ would have him to be. Even conversion, baptism, and church attendance fall short of "absorbing the people into the system." They are in the system but not yet "absorbed" into it. The Bible clearly instructs us to move on to maturity so that we are "no more children, tossed to and fro, and carried about with every wind of doctrine, by the sleight of men, and cunning craftiness" (Ephesians 4:14). We are to be "rooted and built up in him, and stablished in the faith" (Colossians 2:7). But even then we are not fully "absorbed into the system." We must go on to do vital ministry by serving others. A Christian can be mature doctrinally and still be unattached to ministry involvement. Finally, we are to multiply ourselves by evangelizing and discipling others who, in turn, evangelize and disciple others who, in turn…well, you get the picture.

Biblically speaking, I believe assimilation is walking a person through this whole process. True assimilation is completely submerging others into the gospel ministry of the Great Commission and the Great Commandment of our Lord Jesus Christ. Again, God's vision of assimilation stretches our perspective to new challenges and greater expectations.

Absorb into the System

Three main indicators give evidence that a new believer and/or new member has begun the journey into church assimilation. The first is baptism. Baptism is the way a new believer identifies with the death, burial, and resurrection of Jesus Christ. When we are saved, we are joined to Christ as His Bride. Baptism is the Christian's "wedding ring" that gives an outward demonstration of our union with Christ. While it is true you don't have to wear a wedding ring to be married, you wouldn't reject it during the exchanging of rings at your wedding. Can you imagine your spouse telling the officiating minister at your wedding that he/she was not interested in wearing the ring and, in fact, had no inclination to do so throughout the marriage? I doubt that wedding ceremony will ever get to the part where the marriage is sealed with a kiss. Likewise, I have difficulty with those who say they are truly born again but refuse baptism.

The second indicator giving validity to being absorbed into the system is church attendance. Most churches do not require attendance as a membership criteria. Just as baptism identifies one with Christ, church attendance identifies one with the body of Christ. Are a man and woman really living as husband and wife if one refuses to live with the other? If a couple is recognized as being married by sharing a residence together, then it stands to reason others will not acknowledge us as the Bride of Christ if we never go to His house! It is reasonable and natural for the "bride" and the "bridegroom" to be together in the house.

The third indicator giving validity to being assimilated into the church system is Sunday School attendance. Again, most churches do not require Sunday School attendance as a membership criteria; but Sunday School attendance identifies one with the family of God. Sunday School moves the church from a corporate entity in your life to a personal touch on your life. Sunday School is the face and smile the church wears because it puts the church in a more intimate perspective in your life. As a member of the family, we are to be with other family members. Church attendance can provide some of this, but it falls short in providing the intimate relationship building that is a necessary part of family life. Is a member really identifying with a local group of believers if he will not meet with them and interact with them so that he knows them and they know him? Are family members to live in the same house but never speak to one another? Never interact with one another? Never share their heart and life with one another?

Sunday School moves the church from a corporate entity in your life to a personal touch on your life.

Sunday School should take every step to move the church's membership into small-group Bible study. This can be done in three ways. First, implore every class Outreach Leader to systematically contact new members and invite them to Sunday School. Second, assign every unattending church member to a Care Group and have those Care Groups methodically make contacts and touches. Third, design and implement a New Members Class. I suggest you have your New Members Class on Sunday mornings because it usually enhances participation. If a person only comes to church once a week, it is most always on Sunday morning. You also help them develop the habit of attending Sunday School. In your New Members Class, teach them the validity of their Sunday School participation.

A visitor's first-time experience is critical because every time the visitor returns, your chances of reaching him or her doubles. Over half of those who visit three times or more will eventually join. The key is friendliness. People go where they are welcome. If people visit your class and feel they are wanted and the class exudes warmth toward each other, they will probably return unless the teacher bombed on the lesson. Two words best describe friendliness: speaking and smiling. The teacher's interaction with them is important. Remember: People go to the church where they like the pastor, and people attend a particular class because they like the teacher. Teachers are miniature pastors and must, therefore, avail themselves to those attending their class every week; and remember: speak and smile.

Signage and an information/greeter station are strategic in aiding visitors. People should be escorted to their class, not told where it is. Visiting families should be escorted to their individual classes by taking the youngest first and working your way to the oldest. This helps the parents or older siblings know where to retrieve the younger children.

Sunday School rooms should have that "we're expecting company" look. If someone calls my house and informs me they are on the way over and will be there in a few minutes, then I get busy picking up the house. I want to be ready for company.

Sunday School rooms should have that "we're expecting company" look.

When I go to other churches to speak, it is always interesting for me to walk through the church's educational facilities. Many times it is obvious they are not expecting company. The rooms are cluttered and unkept. There is a piano in the corner of the room with all kinds of hymnals, books, and other literature stacked on top of it. One room I was in recently had a poster advertising a four-week Bible study series that was dated eighteen months before. One church had an educational wing with pictures on the walls that had been donated to the church forty-two years earlier. Another church experiencing a real space crunch had a room full of old couches that people had donated to the church (out of the goodness of their hearts, I'm sure). These couches occupied a room that could have accommodated forty to forty-five people but took up so much room that they could only handle twenty. I told them Jesus died for people, not furniture. Make room for the people, and get rid of those old couches that some flea-bitten dog had laid on before they were graciously donated to the church. By the way, furniture, pictures, and other household items should never be donated to or accepted by the church if the item is not acceptable for your living room. If you wouldn't put in your house, then don't put it in God's house!

"To Take into the Mind and Thoroughly Comprehend"

Webster's Dictionary gives a second definition for *assimilate*: "to take into the mind and thoroughly comprehend." If we are to truly assimilate people, then they must think in a manner consistent with the church. Sunday School is the educational ministry of the church that is best suited for this. Sunday School has the greatest opportunity to impact the greatest amount of people on a consistent basis with life-changing Bible study. Sunday School provides "grazing ground" each week as a prepared teacher brings people and the Bible to a crossroads where the two can intersect. Transformation occurs when the Holy Spirit places the infallible Word at the point of people's needs.

Sunday School has the greatest opportunity to impact the greatest amount of people on a consistent basis with life-changing Bible study.

As Bible truth is "taken into the mind and thoroughly comprehended," people will radically conform to the image of Christ.

> "And be not conformed to this world: but be ye transformed by the renewing of your mind, that ye may prove what is that good, and acceptable, and perfect, will of God" (Romans 12:2).

A person's belief system is vital to all he does because the way one believes affects the way he behaves. It is often hard to identify spiritual maturity, but I do believe it encompasses a desire to know what God thinks and what God says. Jesus said we would know a tree by its fruit. (Matthew 7:15-20) An obvious fruit for a Christian would be a study of the Bible so that he can "take into the mind and thoroughly comprehend" it. An obedient child of God should have a hunger for the Word of God.

> "As newborn babes, desire the sincere milk of the word, that ye may grow thereby" (1 Peter 2:2).

A truly born-again person should desire the study of God's Word. My new, little ten-month-old grandson, Braden, has no problem communicating when he is hungry. Furthermore, he goes after that bottle like there will never be another one. Why? It's natural. God made us with the need to eat. In like manner, the Bible says it is natural for born-again believers to desire the "milk of the word." Why is it that so many don't? Maybe they're not really saved.

The New Members Class immediately places new lambs in the church pasture to feed and graze. The New Members Class should teach the church's doctrine, vision, structure, and expectations. New members are so excited about the church. If not, they would have joined another church. This is the perfect time to provide information about the church that they can "take into the mind and thoroughly comprehend." People will not be biblically assimilated until they have experienced transformational thinking. A New Members Class should teach people the importance of the Word of God and how to have a daily quiet time. Every member also needs exposure to the church's major doctrinal positions.

The church will die from the inside if she does not continue to grow disciples, and you cannot grow a disciple apart from the Word of God. I am amazed at some of the Sunday School curriculum that some churches are using. It seems we gravitate to the world's agenda more than we do God's. We implement a lot of "cute" curriculum that may appease people without growing them. The curriculum itself leads people to be self-absorbed instead of God-absorbed and others-absorbed. I had the opportunity to observe one church's curriculum for discipling men. It was almost completely devoid of the Word. My question was and still is: "How do you disciple someone apart from Holy Scripture?" We need to quit toying around with our Sunday School curriculum and feed people milk and meat, not cotton candy.

My question was and still is: "How do you disciple someone apart from Holy Scripture?"

The future of the church depends upon each generation growing the faith of others through the Word of God.

> "So then faith cometh by hearing, and hearing by the word of God" (Romans 10:17).

"Appropriate Them as Nourishment"

When the maturation process has become of age, we should see another of Webster's definitions for *assimilate*: "appropriate them as nourishment." The excitement builds as we progressively assimilate people into the church. They are "absorbed into the system"; then they are "to take into the mind and thoroughly comprehend"; then they are to be "appropriated for nourishment." That which was the recipient of nourishment is now the supplier of it! Those who once needed our nourishment are now feeding others. Can you see the progression of biblical assimilation? It is not God's will for our adults to sit in our classes for years and soak up nourishment. We have enough "pew potatoes" and "spiritual porkers" in our churches as it is. God would have us all to grow to the stage that we are "appropriated as nourishment" for others. Every adult teacher should teach and minister with this in mind. Their goal should be to send many people out of their class for ministry service or involve them within the class in ministry.

Jesus said, "It is more blessed to give than to receive" (Acts 20:35b). Either this is true or it is not. Since we know it is true, we should shove as many adults into service as we possibly can; for this will be best for them. Consistent with Acts 20:35, the happiest people I know in our churches are those who serve. The opposite also is true: Those who are self-absorbed in the church and do not provide nourishment for others are the ones who are usually most critical of the church and hardest to please.

"To Make Similar"

The last definition from Webster's I want to emphasize for our consideration in the assimilation process is: "to make similar." Can you see the progression?

"absorb into the system"

"to take into the mind and thoroughly comprehend"

"appropriate them as nourishment"

"to make similar"

"To make similar" is to reproduce yourself. It is to make others like us or to make others like the church. In speaking to the church at Rome, Paul instructed that once we are saved we are then predestined "to be conformed to the image of his Son" (Romans 8:29). Believers were initially called "disciples" until Acts 11:26 when the Antioch believers were renamed "Christians" which means "a little Christ." So as we follow Christ and become "similar" to Him, we, in essence, lead others who are following us to become more like Christ. It is no wonder Paul could encourage the Thessalonian church to follow him. (2 Thessalonians 3:7-9)

If we are "to make similar," then we must have the right attitude. It is your attitude that impacts people, not your abilities. Abilities impress people; they even help people; but they do not change people.

The attitude of a reproducer is: "a willingness to pour my life into another person and share my life with him, a desire to live for the next generation." A reproducer's attitude will drive his actions. The actions of a reproducer are: "to step into another's life and develop that person as if he had to take your place in life." For this reason, Sunday School teachers should be reproducing themselves and discipling more teachers. Outreach Leaders should be reproducing themselves and developing more Outreach Leaders. Care Group Leaders should step into other people's lives and duplicate more Care Group Leaders.

Every blood-bought Christian should be a reproducer. The teaching of Jesus in John 15 informs us we will produce fruit if we "abide in the Vine." This task is for everyone, not just a select, few "super saints." We cannot all produce the same amount of fruit, but we all can produce fruit. To excuse ourselves from being a reproducer is to deny the power of the Holy Spirit within us. Even vegetation was created with fruit-bearing seed so that all vegetation could reproduce itself. The animal world was created with the same ability. In fact, everything God created with the potential to grow has the ability to reproduce itself. So how can we excuse Christians from doing likewise when we have more life in us than any other created order?

Here are some principles that reproducers need to understand.

- Reproducers need more elimination in their lives, so they can have more concentration in their service.

Our preoccupation with worldliness has been a tremendous deterrent to the cause of the Great Commission. As someone has well said, "Life is like a suitcase. You can only cram so much in it." You cannot do everything, so manage your life by priority. I try to order my life by Matthew 6:33: "But seek ye first the kingdom of God, and his righteousness; and all these things shall be added unto you."

You cannot do everything, so manage your life by priority.

- You reproduce what you are.

You cannot reproduce what you are not; you reproduce what you are. My daughter Angie is exactly like her mother. She looks like Linda's side of the family, and she acts just like Linda. Why? Because Linda reproduced herself. You cannot reproduce what you are not.

- Reproducing is a process, not an event.

The effort to reproduce one's self is an exercise in endurance and patience. It requires perseverance and focus. It will not happen overnight, and you must be committed for the long haul. You cannot attend a seminar and walk away with a completed project. The seminar may help along the way, but to reproduce yourself in someone else will take an investment of life.

To reproduce yourself in someone else will take an investment of life.

- Everyone who makes an impact for God had a mentor.

Joshua had Moses; Elisha had Elijah; Solomon had David; the disciples had Jesus; Paul had Barnabas; Timothy had Paul; etc. We learn from each other. We cannot depend on just our intelligence, education, experiences, and personality. We must have others to step into our lives and make us better than we could be if we were left to nothing but our own devices.

- Developing others is not a classroom issue; it's a life issue!

Simply put, if you are going to reproduce yourself in others, you must be willing to invest your life in them. There are no shortcuts.

Why should we reproduce?

- We are commanded to.

"Go ye therefore, and teach (make disciples) all nations, baptizing them in the name of the Father, and of the Son, and of the Holy Ghost: Teaching them to observe all things whatsoever I have commanded you" (Matthew 28:19-20).

- To stir up the gift of God in others.

"Wherefore I put thee in remembrance that thou stir up the gift of God, which is in thee by the putting on of my hands" (2 Timothy 1:6).

- To support those already serving.

"Two are better than one; because they have a good reward for their labor" (Ecclesiastes 4:9).

- To better serve each other.

"For as we have many members in one body, and all members have not the same office: So we, being many, are one body in Christ, and every one members one of another" (Romans 12:4-5).

- To grow the church spiritually and numerically.

"From whom the whole body fitly joined together and compacted by that which every joint supplieth, according to the effectual working in the measure of every part, maketh increase of the body unto the edifying of itself in love" (Ephesians 4:16).

- To bring glory to God.

"Herein is my Father glorified, that ye bear much fruit; so shall ye be my disciples" (John 15:8).

What are the benefits of reproducing?

- Fulfillment – It builds leaders for tomorrow.

- Strength – It edifies the church today.

- Joy – It expands and multiplies your own ministry.

Mentoring Proverb: "When you are involved in the discipling of another, you double your joy and cut your sorrow in half."

- Love – It establishes a deep and lasting relationship between the disciple and the discipler.

As you can see, assimilating people is like the dating process. It is a gradual, ongoing progression that eventually leads to marriage. As we faithfully assimilate people, we will eventually see our converts loved and discipled to the point of their multiplication in the lives of others. True biblical assimilation starts us out as new converts who are baptized into the church and then set on a course of spiritual discipleship, then service, and ultimately reproduction of themselves in others.

Hand-in-Hand

When a person walks the aisle of our church during the invitation, he takes the pastor's hand and they dialogue about the decision he wants to make for the Lord. The pastor takes the person and hands them off to an altar counselor. But who takes the hand of the new believer/member after that? These new people cannot go on without the attention of the church. We have a responsibility to them. When young parents bring a baby home from the hospital, they do not say,

"Now Junior, here's the kitchen. If you get hungry, feel free to make yourself a peanut butter and jelly sandwich" or "you can use this bathroom since it is close to your room." No, that baby needs constant attention. So it is with new believers and new members. Therefore, we must find a way for the pastor and altar counselor to take their hand and then hand them off. David provided us with a great verse for all reproducers:

"I will instruct thee and teach thee in the way which thou shalt go: I will guide thee with mine eye" (Psalm 32:8).

At our church, we hand them off to our "First Steps" Church Information Class. We have a team that contacts them during the week and invites them to our seven-week class where we "instruct them and teach them in the way that they should go." When they have completed this class, they are handed off to an age-graded Sunday school class. It is our strategy to take their hand, hold it, then pass them on to the next person until they are assimilated into an ongoing Sunday School class.

We have embraced the flowing mission statement for our new member ministry:

To assimilate new members into the life of the church so that the church plays a vital role in their lives and they play a vital role in the life of the church.

As you can see, we are intentional about our responsibility to help them and allow the church to make a difference in their lives. But we are just as intentional about their responsibility to eventually serve in a manner that makes a difference in the church.

This is exactly what Barnabas did for Saul of Tarsus. As a new believer, Saul wanted to gather with other Christians; but they were afraid of him and did not believe he had been really saved. Barnabas "took his hand" and escorted him to the apostles:

> "But Barnabas took him, and brought him to the apostles, and declared unto them how he had seen the Lord in the way, and that he had spoken to him, and how he had preached boldly at Damascus in the name of Jesus. And he was with them coming in and going out at Jerusalem" (Acts 9:27-28).

From this time until we get to Acts 13:43, we see the dynamic duo are always referred to as "Barnabas and Saul." (Acts 11:25, 30; 12:25; 13:1, 2, 7) But from this time forward, they are mostly referred to as "Paul and Barnabas." Barnabas had discipled Paul so well that the mentoree had now risen above the mentor. You may think Barnabas must have been somewhat negligent to have Paul pass him up. On the contrary, I think he did one outstanding job of mentoring his protégé. He reproduced himself. He assimilated Paul into the fellowship of the church so that the church played a vital role in Paul's life. He also assimilated Paul so well that he played a vital role in the church and made a huge difference in others. I tip my hat to Barnabas.

I do not know where the following came from, but it is so good I have to share it with you. As I understand, this quote came from a black pastor speaking to a group of college students:

Children, you are going to die. And one of these days, they are going to take you into a cemetery, drop you into a hole, throw some dirt on your face, go back to the church, and eat potato salad.

When you were born, you alone were crying and everybody else was happy. The important question is this: When you die, are you alone going to be happy leaving everybody else crying? The answer depends on whether you lived to get titles or whether you lived to get testimonies.

When they lay you in the grave, are people going to stand around reciting the fancy titles you earned, or are they going to stand around giving testimonies of the good things you did for them? Will you leave behind just a newspaper column telling people how important you were, or are you going to leave crying people who give testimony of how they lost the best friend they ever had? And nothing's wrong with titles. Those are good things to have. But if it ever comes down to a choice between titles and testimonies, go for the testimonies!

As we biblically assimilate people, we will build testimonies that will outlast us. We will not have merely lived a life; we will have left a legacy!

CORE VALUE
NUMBER SIX:

Building
Relationships
with *People*

CHAPTER 11

United by Relationships

When surveying Sunday School members, I have found the two top reasons they attend are the Bible study and relationships. When I asked why they chose the particular class they attended, they overwhelmingly said things like: "It feels like family"; "The people are so friendly"; "We have many friends in our class"; "The class is so warm"; and "We really love each other." In essence, they are united by relationships. Relationships are the glue that holds the class together. Relationships are the magnet that draws new people to the class. The old cliche has been well used, but it is still true that "people don't care how much you know until they first know how much you care."

When asked what is most important to you, the vast majority of people will not mention a material possession. They will respond by naming a person that is special to them. Materialism can be replaced; people cannot.

Keys to relationship building are commonality, communication, and consistency. Sunday School is fertile ground for all three of these aspects. We have a common purpose in Sunday School to love and accept each other and to focus our attention—and hopefully our lives—around biblical instruction. We have the opportunity to dialogue with each other because Sunday School places us in a small-group setting that is essential for building relationships. Also the privilege to gather each week establishes a consistent pattern of meeting with others. Therefore, Sunday School is critical to a church because it places people in an environment to relationally connect with one another. For this reason, my pastor, Dr. Johnny Hunt, has repeatedly exhorted our people: "If you only attend one hour on Sunday morning, do not come to hear me preach; go to Sunday School." "Big church" is designed to build vertical relationships: man to God. Sunday School is designed to build horizontal relationships: man to man. We need both.

A person must receive more than information at Sunday School; they can stay at home and get that. Modern-day technology affords people the option of staying home and getting all of the biblical information they desire. Television, internet, radio, and books provide more wonderful information than one can consume. If Sunday School is to compete with technology based on information alone, then no one will come to Sunday School. However, if Sunday School competes with technology based on relationships, then technology doesn't have a fighting chance. We can teach instructionally, and certainly there is a need for that. However, real discipleship takes place when we teach relationally. Our example is Jesus Himself. He taught the crowds, but He discipled the Twelve. Why? There was commonality, communication, and consistency. Jesus shared instruction with them, but He also shared His life with them. People must be what drives us. Projects, programs, and presentations will end and grow old; but relationships live forever.

"If you only attend one hour
on Sunday morning, do not come to hear
me preach; go to Sunday School."

I want to once again bring attention to the Care Group ministry that establishes a great platform for relationship building within the class. It is important to understand that relationships set the environment for your class. If the class members are cold, negative, and isolated from each other, then it will be a struggling class of cynicism, mistrust, and little fruit. But if the class members are warm, positive, caring, and interactive with each other, then it will be a thriving class full of excitement, growth, and trust. Relationships mold the environment of the class, and the environment of the class shapes the results of the class. Classes rise and fall on relationships!

Relationships mold the environment of the class, and the environment of the class shapes the results of the class.

Here are ten reasons you need to implement Care Groups in adult classes.

1. To place people in a comfort zone.

I know this sounds strange because most churches are so comfortable that they are stuck. I am not talking about this kind of comfort. Many churches need a good dose of change. Change is vital to the continued progress of any organization. There are many things that must change often: facilities, parking, programming, staff, lay leadership, schedule, multiple services, and Bible study hours, etc. These are good and beneficial to the church for the most part. But among all of the changes that are taking place, there must be some level of comfort and familiarity.

I believe the missing ingredient in most church growth circles is the lack of balance between change and comfort. I have seen some churches change so much so fast that it split the church. Therefore, I believe there must be a balance between change and comfort. I believe change *facilitates* growth. Notice I did not say produces growth. You can change and still not grow. However, you cannot continue to climb to new heights without ever changing. Just as change *facilitates* growth, comfort *stabilizes* growth.

What is the stabilizer in an ever-changing church? Relationships! And where are relationships formed? In Care Groups. The Care Group ministry of a Sunday School class provides the relationship building needed for comfort. Meeting weekly with a group of believers you love and trust will give you a sense of belonging, security, and stability.

What is the stabilizer in an ever-changing church? Relationships!

One night Linda and I had a couple of teachers over to the house for dinner. After the meal, we sat around drinking coffee and enjoying the fellowship. Buddy and Pat Hulsey, longtime Woodstockers, were there; and Buddy asked me, "Allan, how long have you been at the church now?" "Seven years," I replied. I saw a big smile come across his face that stirred my curiosity; so I asked, "Why? What are you thinking about?" "Since you have become our Minister of Education, you have moved my class to another room seven times," he said. Then I smiled back at him and said, "Buddy, do you know how many complaints I have received from your class over these seven years? None!" People usually get attached to "their" room and voice their displeasure when they are asked to move. Why had this class then never voiced a grumble among all of the upheaval? Because they had each other. The change that facilitated our growth was stabilized by the comfort of endearing relationships!

2. To enhance member interaction.

God created us for relationships; He created us with the desire to interact; He created us with the need for self-expression. He had created Adam and placed him in a perfect environment – as no one else has ever experienced. But even in a perfect world, God declared, "It is not good that the man should be alone." This dude needed a dudette! Even in the bliss of the Garden of Eden, Adam needed someone with whom to relate and interact. So God created Eve. When Jesus sent out His missionary teams, He sent them in pairs, not alone. God's design was structured around our need for each other. Intimate relationships are imperative to the health and balance of any person.

Some people argue they are not extroverted and outgoing. This is the evidence they offer as proof they can exist without relationships. They probably can "exist" without them, but they will not thrive without them. It has been proven many times over the detriment of a baby who goes without being touched, talked to, and loved. Babies' personalities may vary, but their need for interaction remains constant. It is true some adults do not need as many relationships as others, but it does not negate anyone's need for some relational interaction.

Again, I want to emphasize: the larger the group, the less interaction. Sunday School is the relational center of the church and must be structured accordingly. We cannot conceptually bypass this fact. This approach will necessitate us having small classes and/or implementing the Care Group ministry within a class set-up that provides for Care Group interaction. To ignore this is to do nothing more than relegate

Sunday School to an age-graded worship service. Openness and sharing are natural in small groups.

Sunday School is the relational center of the church and must be structured accordingly.

A side benefit of interacting with others is the help it lends in overcoming teachers who always lecture and never provide opportunity for people to express themselves. If class members have time in a Care Group to express themselves and to interact with others, then it takes some of the sting out of their inability to do so during the Bible study time. This should not excuse the teacher from using different teaching methodologies, but it will help lessen the frustration to class members when he does not.

3. To develop relationships.

I believe the greatest hindrance to relationship building is affluency. I have been "marked" by my childhood days. My dad left home when I was five years old; and we moved in with Granny, and Mom had to go to work. We were financially poor but family rich. My mom had six sisters and one brother. Six of those girls lived within a two-block radius of our house. I had so many cousins to play with that I didn't need friends. After supper each night, we would sit around and talk, tell stories, and the like. We might decide to watch one of the three TV channels (NBC, CBS, and if the aluminum foil was just right on the rabbit ears, we could get ABC) available to us on our little black-and-white television. In warm weather, we would sit on the big front porch with aunts, uncles, cousins, and neighbors and just enjoy each other. Much of my philosophy of life was formed on that porch as I heard many topics discussed by those I loved. I received a lot of "relational instruction" sitting in that old, squeaky swing. We were poor, so materialism could not become a barrier to our relationship building.

Some time back, I came home from the office and Linda was in the kitchen preparing supper. I asked where the kids were and discovered they were in the house. I went to one room and found Kelly and Angie watching television. When I asked why they weren't watching TV in the family room (that is open to the kitchen), they replied they didn't want to watch what Linda had on. I then found Jake playing Nintendo in his room. I asked him the same question and got the same answer. So I told all three of them to go to the family room and hang out with their mother and I. They did reluctantly. I then made the comment to all of them: "Do you know what our problem is? We have been too blessed of God. We have so many gadgets and don't need each other." At one time, we even established Tuesday night as "Family Night"; and we did everything together that night with no other interruptions.

I have had the God-blessed opportunity to minister abroad in some former communist countries where the average monthly income is forty to sixty dollars a month. I have stayed in the homes of pastors in Romania, Ukraine, Hungary, and the former U.S.S.R. After supper the family does not spread out and go their separate ways. They sit together at the dinner table and talk about their day and life in general. They do not have televisions, computers, Gameboys, etc., as we do. All they have is each other! How refreshing it was to sit around the table each night and just share life with one another.

4. To develop intimacy.

If we are placing people in a comfort zone, if we are allowing for interaction and relationship development, then we will experience intimate relationships among our class members. Intimacy happens when emotional bonding has taken place. I'm not talking about a sexual bonding or intimacy; I'm referring to a true, spiritual *koinonia*. *Strong's Exhaustive Concordance* defines *koinonia* as "social intercourse." It is a strong bond between two people much like David and Jonathan had.

I have seen this over and over again at our church. We are a large church, but the fellowship is even larger. Time would not allow me to tell you of the ministry that takes place within the established relationship of Sunday School classes and Care Groups. Our people really take care of one another, and it happens within the structure and relationships of Sunday School. In fact, Sunday School is our plan to meet people's needs; and we have no "Plan B."

Difficulties are life's common denominator. Everyone is, has, and will experience difficulty and heartache of some kind. Therefore, the human race is interconnected and can relate to the pain and suffering that is inevitably ours.

Feelings are at the heart of life. Because of our commonality in dealing with hurt, we can all sympathize with others. Christians, prompted by the love and compassion of Christ, have heartstrings that attach us to those in difficulty.

5. To assimilate new members.

People are naturally assimilated where they have relationships. It is not our managerial skills that will drive our assimilation process; it is our relational skills. People go where they are loved, not where they

*People go where they are loved,
not where they are directed.*

are directed. As someone has said, "Insincerity has a strong odor; and sooner or later, everyone's bound to catch a whiff of it."

6. To follow up on visitors.

Good relationships with our class members will encourage them to treat prospects correctly. And when prospects are treated right, they will come back. If the member knows he is cared for, he will have no problem sharing that with others. Placing visitors in Care Groups starts the relationship development process. It also starts the follow-through process as members start contacting those they are beginning to know. If we do not follow up on our visitors, then we are worse than a real estate agent who does not follow up on a client who wants to buy a house and has money. By attending your church and/or class, people make a statement that they have some interest.

7. To provide a caring ministry.

Here is a good principle: To handle yourself, use your head; to handle others, use your heart. If we are to care for others, we must have a heart. We must exercise compassion. Care Groups are designed to know people's needs and then to meet those needs. Care Groups provide the organization for ministering to people's needs.

Recently, my pastor shared with me that a young couple who had lost an infant child called him and said, "Our Sunday School class has been so good to us. We didn't want to hurt their feelings, but could you please inform them to not bring any more food? We have more than we will ever eat!" Another class literally ran another class member's business while he was in the hospital battling leukemia. One man tearfully shared with me that his newborn baby had colic and kept them up at night. This couple had other children as well. Between their jobs and children, they were exhausted. So different people from their class came over several consecutive nights and stayed up with their baby until they could get rested up.

8. To contact absentees.

Everyone needs to know they are loved and cared for. A contact by a concerned Care Group member says, "We care for you and missed you." It is unrealistic to expect the teacher to keep up with everyone who misses and then contact them. The Care Group structure provides the perfect mechanism to know who is missing and then to assign that person to a concerned member who will follow up on the absentee.

9. To hold each other accountable.

Care Groups allow us to hold each other accountable because our relationship has earned us the right to do so. When I was coaching, I never went home at night without calling the home of any player who missed practice. I needed to know his status. My call showed concern, and it also held my players accountable to our expectations.

10. To keep the church small.

Everyone wants to attend a growing, vibrant, on-fire, soul-winning, life-changing, small church! So let's give it to them. We can grow larger and smaller all at the same time. As the church reaches more people and grows larger and larger, it also gets smaller and smaller by placing people into Sunday School classes and Care Groups. When people say they want to attend a small church, what they are really saying is they want friendship, warmth, and a family atmosphere. I agree with them; this is the kind of church I want; and I have found Sunday School gives me this – regardless of the size church I am attending.

The largeness of a church becomes increasingly irrelevant to people as long as their needs are being met. In fact, a small church will not retain people if their needs are unnoticed. The feeling of genuine love and care will eventually erase the anxiety of the size of the organization. Churches cannot afford to outgrow their concern and compassion for the people. How does a person become great? By doing the little things. Likewise, a church becomes great by doing the little things.

The largeness of a church becomes
increasingly irrelevant to people
as long as their needs are being met.

Relationships are the connecting agent that holds us together.

"Ye also, as lively stones, are built up a spiritual house, a holy priesthood, to offer up spiritual sacrifices, acceptable to God by Jesus Christ" (1 Peter 2:5).

As "living stones," our relationships are the mortar that bond us together. As John Fawcett wrote many years ago:

> *Blest be the tie that binds*
>
> *Our hearts in Christian love;*
>
> *The fellowship of kindred minds*
>
> *Is like to that above.*

I hope you noticed that one word was present in each of the Six Core Values: *People.* Sunday School is in the people business. In fact, if there were no people, God would have no purpose for your Sunday School! It really is true: God loves people more than anything. I trust a look at these *Six Core Values of Sunday School* will help your Sunday School love people as God does.

APPENDIX 1

Sunday School Covenant

Read carefully the following covenant. Check the appropriate line for each statement. Please sign and date at the bottom if you wish to join yourself to a group of leaders committed to ministry.

	Yes	No

1. I have a personal relationship with God through Jesus Christ.

_____ _____

2. I feel called of God to serve Him through the Sunday School.

_____ _____

3. I will strive to follow the leadership of the Holy Spirit.

_____ _____

4. I will *actively participate in training and growing opportunities.

_____ _____

5. I will *actively participate in reaching lost and unchurched persons.

_____ _____

6. I will *actively participate in Sunday School Leadership Meetings.

_____ _____

7. I will do all I can to make Sunday mornings a positive, uplifting experience. _____ _____

8. I will be faithful in tithing (giving 10 percent of my gross earnings).

_____ _____

9. I will completely refrain from the use of alcoholic beverages.

_____ _____

Yes   No

10. I will attend Sunday morning and evening worship services and Wednesday evening activities unless providentially hindered.

_____   _____

11. I will be supportive of the Pastor and staff.   _____   _____

12. I have read and agree with the church's Sunday School Philosophy and will lead my class according to it.   _____   _____

Before my Lord Jesus Christ, I commit myself to serve Him and His church by faithfully ministering through the Sunday School of First Baptist Church, Woodstock, Georgia.

_____

Sign

_____

Date

* "actively participate" means you will be involved unless providentially hindered.

APPENDIX 2

Truths We Hold Dear

"Not many of you should presume to be teachers, my brothers, because you know that we who teach will be judged more strictly" (James 3:1, NIV).

Name   _____

Position   _____

It is our desire to have those presenting the Word of God to be in agreement with the church's position on our essential beliefs. The following represents those beliefs. Please circle the number that best represents your conviction for each doctrinal statement.

1.– Strongly Agree   2. – Mostly Agree   3. – Somewhat Agree

4.– Somewhat Disagree   5. – Mostly Disagree   6. – Strongly Disagree

1. About God: God is the Creator and Ruler of the universe. He has eternally existed in three persons: the Father, the Son, and Holy Spirit. These three are co-equal and are one God.

     1   2   3   4   5   6

2. About the Father: He is all powerful, all knowing, all loving, and all wise. He reigns with providential care over the universe and the flow of human history goes according to His purposes and plan.

     1   2   3   4   5   6

3. About Jesus: Jesus Christ is the Son of God. He is co-equal with the Father. Jesus has eternally existed and became man at His incarnation. He lived a sinless human life and offered Himself as the perfect sacrifice for the sins of all people by dying on a cross. He bodily arose from the dead after three days to demonstrate His power

over sin and death. He ascended to Heaven's glory and will return again someday to earth to reign as King of Kings and Lord of Lords.

1   2   3   4   5   6

4. About the Holy Spirit: He is the third person of the Trinity. He guides men into all truth; exalts Christ; convicts of sin, righteousness, and judgment; cultivates Christian character; comforts believers; bestows spiritual gifts by which believers serve God; and seals the believer unto the day of final redemption. His presence in the lives of believers is the assurance of God to bring us into the fullness of the stature of Christ.

1   2   3   4   5   6

5. About Scriptures: The Bible is God's Word to us. It was written by human authors, under the supernatural guidance of the Holy Spirit. It is the supreme source of truth for Christian beliefs and living. Because it is inspired by God, it has salvation for its end and is truth without any mixture of error.

1   2   3   4   5   6

6. About Human Beings: People are made in the image of God and are the supreme object of God's creation. All of us are marred by an attitude of disobedience toward God called sin. Sin separates people from God and causes many problems in life.

1   2   3   4   5   6

7. About Salvation: Salvation is God's free gift to us, but we must accept it. We can never make up for our sin by self-improvement or good works. Only by trusting Jesus Christ as God's offer of forgiveness can anyone be saved from sin's penalty. When we turn from our self-ruled life and turn to Jesus in faith, we are saved. Eternal life begins the moment one receives Jesus Christ into his life by faith.

1   2   3   4   5   6

8. About Eternal Security: Because God gives us eternal life through

Jesus Christ, the true believer is secure in that salvation for eternity. If you have been genuinely saved, you cannot "lose" your salvation. Salvation is maintained by the grace and power of God, not by the self-effort of the Christian. It is the grace and keeping power of God that gives us this security

1   2   3   4   5   6

9. About Eternity: People were created to exist forever. We will either exist eternally separated from God by sin or eternally with God through forgiveness and salvation. To be eternally separate from God is Hell. To be eternally in union with Him is eternal life. Heaven and Hell are real places of eternal existence.

1   2   3   4   5   6

10. About Baptism by Immersion: We believe that scriptural baptism must be: (1) by being completely immersed under the water and (2) after salvation. Jesus was immersed, and all baptisms in the New Testament were by immersion. These two facts set the standard for baptism today. Baptism has no saving power but is the first act of obedience symbolizing (1) the believer's faith in the death, burial, and resurrection of Jesus; (2) the believer's death to sin and resurrection to walk anew in Christ; and (3) the Christian's belief that he will die, be buried, and that Jesus will resurrect him from the dead.

1   2   3   4   5   6

11. About the Lord's Supper: The Lord's Supper is a symbolic act of obedience whereby believers remember the death of the Lord Jesus and anticipate His second coming. The bread is symbolic of His body and the juice represents His blood.

1   2   3   4   5   6

12. About Tithing: We believe in giving the tithe – ten percent of our gross income (not net income) – as the biblical standard of giving. The tithe is to be given as an undesignated offering to the "storehouse" ministry of a local church. According to the Scriptures, we

are to give cheerfully, regularly, systematically, proportionately, and liberally for the advancement of the Redeemer's cause on earth.

    1   2   3   4   5   6

13. About Evangelism: It is the duty of every born-again follower of Jesus Christ and of every church to endeavor to make disciples of all men everywhere. It is the command of Christ for every believer to seek constantly to win the lost to Christ by personal effort and by all other methods in harmony with the gospel of Christ.

    1   2   3   4   5   6

14. About the Church: A New Testament church of the Lord Jesus Christ is a local body of baptized believers who are associated by their common faith and fellowship with Jesus. A local church is to observe the two ordinances: (1) baptism and (2) the Lord's Supper. The church should exercise their God-given gifts and extend the gospel to the ends of the earth. The church is an autonomous body serving under the Lordship of Christ. All members are equally responsible as they serve with the scriptural officers of the church, the pastors, and deacons.

    1   2   3   4   5   6

15. About Christian Unity: To live in harmony with other believers is clearly the teaching of the New Testament. It is the responsibility of each believer to endeavor to live in fellowship with each member of the congregation. It is further the responsibility of each member to bring all gossiping and backbiting to an end.

    1   2   3   4   5   6

APPENDIX 3

My Personal Testimony

Please use the following questions as a guide to share your testimony with me. Please use the back of the page, or attach another paper to this one if you need more space.

Name _____ Date _____

Date of Salvation _____ Date of Baptism _____

Were you baptized after you were saved? _____ Yes _____ No

Were you baptized by immersion? _____ Yes _____ No

1. What my life was like before I received Christ.

2. How I knew I needed Christ.

3. What took place when I received Christ.

4. How my life has been different since Jesus saved me.

APPENDIX 4

Annual Sunday School Teacher Evaluation

Please answer the following questions honestly. Then set up an appointment with your age-division leader to discuss these issues. The purpose of this evaluation is to draw us closer together as co-laborers in purpose and in heart.

Name   _____

Position   _____

Date   _____

1. What is the purpose of your class?

2. What would you like to see happen in your class? By what date?

3. What is your greatest passion for ministry?

4. If you could do anything with your class this year, what would it be?

5. How are your class and personnel structured around the three tasks of the Sunday School?

   • Reaching People

   • Teaching People

   • Ministering to People

6. How can we help you become a better teacher?

7. How can we help you become a better leader?

8. How can we help you become a better discipler?

9. How can we help you become a better soul-winner?

10. How can we help your class reproduce itself and start new classes?

11. How can we make the ongoing Sunday School Leadership Meetings more effective in helping/equipping you?

12. What topics would you like to see addressed at the Sunday School Leadership Meetings?

13. What other thoughts would you like to share with me that this evaluation has not addressed?

14. How would you rate yourself in the following areas: (1 is low, 5 is high)

A) Actively participating in evangelistic efforts.
 1 2 3 4 5

B) Actively participating in Leadership Meetings.
 1 2 3 4 5

C) Making Sunday morning a positive, uplifting experience.
 1 2 3 4 5

D) Actively participating in training and growth opportunities.
 1 2 3 4 5

E) Developing new leaders from your class.
 1 2 3 4 5

F) Organizing your class for effective ministry.
 1 2 3 4 5

G) Providing excellence in the learning/teaching process of the Bible.
 1 2 3 4 5

H) Giving of the tithe (ten percent of gross income).
 1 2 3 4 5

15. What can you do to improve in each of these areas?

A) _____

B) _____

C) _____

D) _____

E) _____

F) _____

G) _____

H) _____